A Room with a Pew

Let everyone who comes be received as Christ.

—Rule of St. Benedict

☩

I have desired to go
Where springs not fail,
To fields where flies no sharp and sided hail
And a few lilies blow.

And I have asked to be
Where no storms come,
Where the green swell is in the havens dumb,
And out of the swing of the sea.

—"Heaven-Haven: A Nun Takes the Veil"
by Gerard Manley Hopkins (1844–1889)

☩

When a police officer stops a monk for speeding, he smells alcohol on the monk's breath and sees an empty wine bottle on the floor of the car.

"Have you been drinking, sir?" he says.

"Only water," says the monk, his fingers crossed.

"Then why do I smell wine?"

The monk looks at the empty bottle and says, "Good Lord! He must have done it again!"

A Room with a Pew

SLEEPING OUR WAY THROUGH
SPAIN'S ANCIENT MONASTERIES

RICHARD STARKS and MIRIAM MURCUTT

LYONS PRESS
Guilford, Connecticut
An imprint of Globe Pequot Press

Lyons Press is an imprint of Globe Pequot Press.

Project editor: David Legere
Design: Sheryl P. Kober
Layout artist: Sue Murray

Illustrations by Elise Spacek © Morris Book Publishing, LLC

Library of Congress Cataloging-in-Publication data is available on file.

ISBN 978-0-7627-8145-4

Printed in the United States of America

10 9 8 7 6 5 4 3 2 1

Authors' Note

This book has two authors but for the most part it is written in the first-person singular. To have used the first-person plural would have been clumsy. It would also have implied that we are somehow joined at the hip—which, of course, we are not.

Richard Starks
Miriam Murcutt

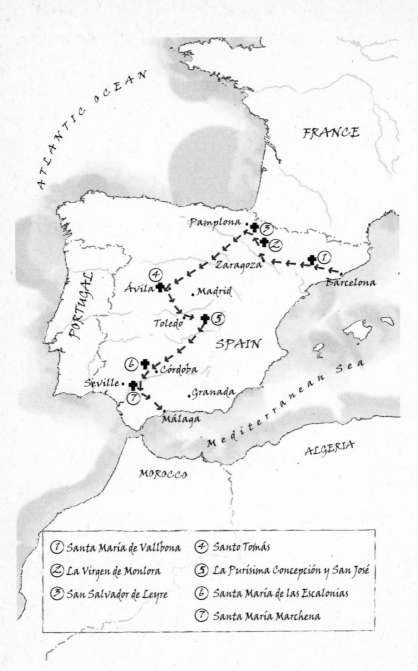

① Santa María de Vallbona   ④ Santo Tomás

② La Virgen de Monlora   ⑤ La Purísima Concepción y San José

③ San Salvador de Leyre   ⑥ Santa María de las Escalonias

                            ⑦ Santa María Marchena

Contents

Introduction

I've never seen a severed finger before. This one, when I examine it closely, is unnaturally long, as if it possesses an extra knuckle. It's also brown, what I would call "formaldehyde brown," the color laboratory specimens turn once they're past their sell-by date. It sticks up in what might be construed as a rude gesture, set like a spent candle in an ornate filigree holder. The blackened nail with its sliver of crescent moon above the cuticle appears to be brittle and badly in need of a trim.

"Her ring finger, was it?" I ask. "From the right hand?"

The man who's showing it to me nods. He doesn't say anything for a moment as we put our heads together and gaze through the glass that contains this holy relic, but perhaps he notices something in my expression. "Don't worry," he adds. "She was dead when they cut it off. So there wouldn't have been any pain."

I'm glad about that, because for the past few weeks I've seen a lot of pain. I've seen men flayed alive, burned at the stake, shot full of arrows, and run through with spears. I've seen heads on platters, entrails on the ground, and tortured souls begging for mercy as hordes of demons pitchfork them into an eternity of Hell. And most nights I've slept in a room with a man nailed to a cross, blood coursing from an open wound in his side, his crowned head lolling onto one shoulder or thrown back as he gazes skyward in anguished rebuke.

It's been a fun-filled few weeks.

Christianity must surely be one of the world's most violent religions—especially when you see it up close from inside a Spanish monastery. It can also, of course, be an inspiration—and, if you approach it with a modicum of doubt, even an inadvertent source of amusement.

"The fingernail," I tell the man beside me. "It needs a trim."

"I know," he says, then flashes a wide conspirator's grin, the kind you might see on a child. "But I'm not allowed to touch it. I'd be roasted alive if I ever did that."

I turn to look at him and for the first time I realize that he's not what I thought. He, too, is a skeptic. Maybe even a non-believer.

He may have been put in charge of the finger. But like me, he's never been handed the gift of faith.

El Reial Monestir de
Santa María de Vallbona

✠

Cistercian

{ONE}

EACH YEAR, NEARLY SIXTY MILLION TOURISTS DESCEND ON SPAIN, most of them headed for one or other of the three Costas—Brava, Blanca, and Sol. These Costas are infamous for their tacky bars and stacked beaches, and in the case of Sol (the most southerly one) for their British-ex-pat, underworld residents.

We're also headed that way, but we're hoping to avoid the crush and the crowds (and the bank robbers and drug dealers, too). Our aim is to start near Barcelona in the northeast, then wend our way south and west past Madrid, Córdoba, and Seville before arriving on the southern Mediterranean coast at Málaga. We'll be following a route that, although inland, we have come to think of as the "Costa del Soul"—a term we've coined to reflect the fact that we plan to stay only in monasteries.

Spain's ancient monasteries will, we are sure, not just provide a novel form of accommodation. They will also give us an intriguing glimpse into another way of life—one that's pursued by a dwindling breed of monks and nuns cloistered within what are essentially living museums of history, culture, and art.

With this plan in mind, we fly into Gerona, one of three airports to serve Barcelona, and pick up a rental car—a blue Fiat Panda with five forward gears and a lawn-mower engine. We squeeze in, jerk the clutch a few times, then drive south on a toll road that parallels the overcrowded coast. Because Spanish monasteries are new to us, we plan to ease ourselves into their medieval way of life by spending our first night in Sant Marcal—an eleventh-century Benedictine monastery that has been transformed into a commercially run hotel, operated under license by a Spanish chain called Husa. We've no idea what it will be like, but since the monastery-hotel bills itself as "a small palace of quietly exquisite taste," where visitors can enjoy a "staff-to-guest ratio of one-to-one," I'm confident we'll be able to take it in stride.

Near the town of Sant Celoni, we leave the highway and head inland toward El Montseny—a large massif that is all but ignored by the tourist hordes on the beaches. Right away we enter what I think of as the "real Spain"—small, isolated villages set in rolling fields uniformly striped with olive trees. As we climb the eastern slope of the massif, the temperature drops and the vegetation begins to change. Cork oak and pinewood give way to groves of beech and fir. A thin mist swirls around us as the road twists and turns, seemingly uncertain of the best way to go.

With night coming on, I'm impatient to arrive, but as the Panda wrestles with another pretzel bend, our cell phone rings and we hear Señor Balsells, Sant Marcal's manager, calling to say that we no longer have a room.

"But we made a reservation," I tell him.

"Sí. I know. But the hotel is now closed."

"But we only booked it a week ago."

"Yes. But now it is closed."

I try to get him to elaborate, but when he expands on "closed," it's only to say that the hotel is "not open."

"I've found you a room elsewhere," he says, and names a sister hotel that Husa operates a few miles on. "You can stay there, and tomorrow I will come to say sorry."

The next day as promised, Señor Balsells tracks us down and finds us eating a late breakfast. He's a fidgety man, about forty years old, who apologizes again in better-than-passable English. He lives, he says, a few miles north in a town called Vich—or Vic, if you prefer its Catalán name.

"Not in Sant Marcal?" I ask him.

He shakes his head. San Marcal is too isolated, he says. There is nothing there except the monastery, now operating as a hotel. Which is closed, he tells us, because no one wants to stay overnight. Just us. Which means he's been forced to tell the one-to-one staff to stay home.

"It's only for a few days," he says, then adds, "I hope."

The hotel is suffering because in a newly austere Spain, corporations no longer book conferences during the week and Spanish lovers no longer hold trysts on the weekends.

"If things don't improve," he says, "we may have to close for good."

The problem, he explains, is that Sant Marcal, although a hotel, is still a monastery owned by the Church. It's part of a portfolio of real estate investments, and the Church, Señor Balsells says, has negotiated a contract that's aimed at generating a steady cash flow.

"We pay them the same rent if business is up or if business is down. It makes no difference to them. But for us"—he shrugs and spreads his hands wide—"we still have other expenses. So if business is down, we're forced to suffer a loss."

He pauses for a moment.

"I think," he says, "that the Church is smarter than we are. But then," he adds, "it has been around a whole lot longer, too."

✠

I used to think that monasteries were started by saints and other benevolent types who were eager to build something tangible for the glory of God. That sometimes happened, of course, but in this part of Spain many of the monasteries were founded by people driven by far more cynical and self-serving motives. As often as not, the monasteries were founded by kings and nobles who donated the land (and sometimes a sizable chunk of cash to go with it) because in exchange they received from the Church absolution for their many sins as well as an affirmation of their right to rule here on Earth. They knew, too, that if they helped build a monastery they would secure for themselves a place to park unmarried daughters, widowed wives, and bastard children—and a place where they could be interred, surrounded by a pious community that would pray for their souls. To the kings and nobles, it seemed like a worthwhile investment, but to minimize their costs, the canny royals usually gave land that they didn't want—or didn't even own—which often meant land that was somewhere off in the middle of nowhere.

Armed with this knowledge, we circle around the town of Manresa to pick up the A2 highway, but then deviate from our route to seek out a *supermercado*. If, for our first true monastery, we're about to head into the wilds, we want to be sure we're well stocked with what, to us, are the essentials of life. At a Mercadona—Spain's ubiquitous supermarket chain—we load up the Panda with olives, cheese, crackers, bread, peaches and pears, two tins of tuna, three tins of sardines, four bottles of *tempranillo*, a six-pack of San Miguel beer, and a small bottle of Amontillado sherry. It's enough food and drink to guarantee that we need never be hungry, thirsty, or sober again.

Then we step back in time, leaving the gas stations and truck stops to enter a world of vineyards, orchards, and stubbled fields of harvested corn. At a deserted crossroads, we pause briefly then head into the sun to follow a road that tracks the course of a meandering stream. The whisper of a breeze stirs the grass by the side of the road, but nothing else moves as we putter along, passing the tiny settlements of Nalec, Rocafort, and Sant Martí. Near Maldà, we dip into the Maldanell Valley, then round a bend and suddenly, profiled against a clear blue sky, there it is: El Reial Monestir de Santa María de Vallbona. The Royal Monastery of Santa María de Vallbona.

It's impossible to miss. The monastery looms over the town of Vallbona de les Monges the way Dracula's castle must have towered above the Transylvanian landscape. Which is not surprising—because until the mid-sixteenth century, the Royal Monastery *was* the town of Vallbona.

For four hundred years—following its founding in 1153—the Royal Monastery of Santa María stood in splendid isolation with no other buildings for miles around. At first it housed a mixed group of Benedictine monks and nuns, but in 1175 the monks moved out, leaving only the nuns, who then switched Orders to become Cistercians. The nuns were the lucky recipients of generous gifts and inheritances from local royals and other big-wigs—especially after they started a school for the daughters of Catalonia's most distinguished families. By the fourteenth century, the monastery was an affluent community with more than 150 nuns enclosed within it.

But then came the Council of Trent—a reformist body that was meant to redeem a Catholic Church that, by the sixteenth century, had become thoroughly corrupt, exhibiting the sexual mores of a Casanova and the moral probity of a Goldman Sachs. Among the numerous topics the Council addressed was the vulnerability of isolated nuns who, "without any protection, were often exposed to the rapacity and other crimes of evil men"— usually priests and bishops, but sometimes the occasional passing Pope. Henceforth, the Council decreed, all nuns in isolated communities would be rounded up—forcibly if need be—and relocated to "monasteries within cities or more populous towns."

Large numbers of "female monasteries" (as they were called) were compelled to close. But El Reial Monestir de Santa María de Vallbona—although occupied entirely by nuns—was able to survive, mainly because of its political clout and the considerable wealth it had acquired by way of its royal connections. The nuns were not made to move to a town. Instead a town was brought to them—the town of Vallbona de les Monges. We can see it now, its tiny houses nestling against the monastery's walls like goslings surrounding a mother goose.

✠

We drive into the center and park in a small empty square. A faded advertisement on a nearby wall extols the virtues of extra virgin olive oil. Next to that is a cafe, its doors closed, blinds drawn. In the opposite corner, a kiosk offers local information, but it, too, is sealed tight. There is no sound except for the knocking of the Panda's engine as it cools, and no sign of life other than a pigeon pecking disconsolately at the grit in a gutter.

We trudge up a cobbled lane past shuttered houses—whose sandstone walls throw back what's left of the sun's heat—and find a church. Its walls are pitted as if they've been raked by machine-gun fire. Statues eroded like melted candles flank the main door, and along one wall a row of sarcophagi rest on short stubby legs. They look abandoned—as if they've been dumped down by medieval removal men and then left there for eight hundred years until a committee decides where they should finally go.

The church door is locked, but a blue sign bolted to a wall directs us towards *el monasterio*. We follow its arrow to the doors of the monastery—two huge slabs of oak heavily studded with iron and held in place by rusted hinges the size of broadswords. They are at the top of a short flight of flagstone steps that have been worn into a bow by nearly one thousand years of penitent feet. The doors are open a crack. We climb up and squeeze between them into the gloom of the entranceway.

As our eyes slowly adjust, we spot a small push-button bell on the wall to our right beneath a typed label that says *portería*. I press on the bell, but nothing happens. I'm beginning to think the Black Death might have returned to kill off everyone who lived here, when a disembodied voice comes out of the wall through a speakerphone next to the label. The voice is distorted, as if it's traveled through static from the other side of the moon, and I can't tell if it belongs to a man or a woman. I lean into the speakerphone and announce in my clearest Spanish, *"Tenemos una reservación."*—We have a reservation. It seems a strange statement to make in this setting, but I haven't yet mastered the art of checking into a Spanish monastery.

We wait again, longer this time, until a small wooden door creaks open and out steps a nun from central casting—sallowfaced, about sixty years old, with thick, round, wire-rimmed glasses. Her long white habit sweeps the floor, and she has a few tufts of frizzy hair peeking out from under the black cloth of her veil. I have several Spanish expressions ready to greet her, but when I try to use one she waggles a finger to indicate I should be quiet. I think I've violated some monastic law that mandates silence, but a few gestures later I realize the nun is telling me she can't understand a word I'm saying because she doesn't speak Spanish—only Catalán. This may be a victory for regional autonomy, but it wipes out weeks of trying to memorize ice-breaker Spanish phrases that have a religious slant.

The nun beckons us up a short flight of steps—a spiral one that leads to another closed door. Out comes a ring of keys. She selects one the size of a crowbar and uses it to open the door. We follow her in and immediately we're hit in the face by a powerful smell of rising damp, like the stench of an English basement. It's also pitch-black, but before stepping into the void, the nun gropes around on the wall to her left and flicks on a light. The room we are in is huge, with a lofty ceiling and stuccoed walls that are hung with paintings of doleful saints suffering through a grisly series of biblical tortures. Two or three tables have been plunked down apparently at random on the stone floor, and along one wall there's a row of overstuffed, papal-size chairs.

The nun strides towards a staircase on the other side of the room. Halfway there, she suddenly accelerates until she is almost running. As I try to keep pace, I realize the light must be on a timer so we need to reach the stairs before we're again plunged into darkness. We follow her up to the second floor and push through an etched-glass door that swings shut behind us, mercifully sealing off the smell of the damp.

The nun steers us along a windowless corridor with closed doors leading off to the left and right. She stops outside one and produces another large key—this one on a velvet-trimmed fob. She unlocks the door of the cell that will be our home for the next few days, and as she ushers us in I think, Thank God (if there is one) for the Panda outside—all stocked up and ready to roll, should we feel the need to make an escape.

☩

At one time, there were literally thousands of monasteries in Spain—many of them founded in the eleventh, twelfth, and thirteenth centuries, when armies of Christians roamed the land, often along pilgrimage routes linked to the Way of St. James, which runs from the Pyrenees in the northeast to Santiago de Compostela in the northwest. These monasteries were built not just to house the growing numbers of resident monks and nuns, but also to bed and breakfast the overnight crowds of itinerant pilgrims. They were, as a result, large, solid, and intended to last.

These days, the demand for their facilities has all but collapsed. A lot of the monasteries have, too, yet many of them remain—still solid, and still able to cater to large numbers of people. It makes sense, therefore, to fill them with some of the new travelers roaming the land—tourists. Until now, this has seemed like a match made in heaven, and one that we might be able to exploit. But as the nun leads us into our cell, I'm beginning to have serious doubts.

We stumble in behind her, still in the dark. The air in the cell is stagnant and cold, until the nun feels her way across the room to throw open a pair of floor-to-ceiling shutters and then a couple of tall French windows. And suddenly the room is transformed. Blinding white light floods in, along with a warming gust of fresh country air. Through the open windows, I can look out at the upper floors of the houses opposite and see scarlet geraniums spilling in waterfalls of color from window boxes perched on every sill.

The nun hands us the key and silently departs with just a swish of her habit. Left on our own, we look around. The cell—or room—is not large, but it is certainly spacious enough. There are two cot-like beds, narrow and firm, with wooden headboards fixed to the walls behind them. Each is covered by a pea-green counterpane with a pillow at the head and a short stack of neatly folded towels at the foot. The sheets are freshly laundered, ironed to a crisp, and smell faintly of newly cut lemons.

Two bedside tables match the chairs and plain wooden desk that stand against the opposite wall. A modern crucifix hangs over the desk, bearing a suffering Jesus who's neatly dressed in a long brown tunic. His feet poke out from under the hem and his arms, of course, are spread wide. There's a New Testament on the corner of the desk along with a medieval image of Madonna and Child, which has been pasted onto a small pyramid of wood. I'm sure that it's here at this desk we're expected to sit and think deep thoughts, but in my mind's irreverent eye the desktop has already become a deli counter mounded with cheese, olives, tuna, and bread, as well as a bottle or two of (unconsecrated) wine that we'll need to bring in from the Panda.

There's a standard lamp in a corner. The tiled floor sparkles with polish. A built-in cupboard provides more than enough space for our clothes. And as for the bathroom—and yes, there is one en suite—it is equipped with a shower, washbasin, and dazzling white toilet. There is no wicker basket full of free-gift soaps and sample shampoos, but that frill aside, the room has everything we need. And *only* what we need. It's plain, simple, uncluttered, and clean—a perfect example of what I think is the Cistercian ideal of "enough."

As an unexpected bonus, a sign on the back of the door gives a room rate of nineteen euros per person per night (twenty-two if we want heat), dropping to fifteen euros (nineteen with heat) if we stay more than one night. By way of comparison, an overnight stay in the monastery-hotel of Sant Marcal (had it been open) would have set us back nearly 120 euros.

{TWO}

THE NEXT MORNING, WE ARRANGE TO MEET SISTER MARÍA FEDERICA. We do this because we're keen to meet a resident nun—any nun. We're not sure how to proceed since the Cistercians here are clois-tered and therefore inaccessible; so we just press the *portería* bell and ask the disembodied voice if we can chat with a nun who speaks Spanish, and Sister María is the one nominated by her abbess to step forward and represent her Order. She agrees to meet us later that day.

At the appointed hour, we again ring the *portería* bell and Sister María invites us into a part of the monastery that's nor-mally off limits to outsiders. She leads us into the cloister, but then doubles back on a circuitous route and takes us into the room that—from the damp and the dark—I recognize as the one we passed through when we first arrived. This, I think, is the *locu-torium*—the monastic equivalent of a Victorian parlor, where visi-tors are taken if a nun wishes to meet with them.

Sister María fiddles with the switch that turns on the light (and hopefully turns off the timer) and we settle into the papal-size chairs that have now been drawn up to one of the large oak tables. Sister María cannot be more than five feet tall, so dwarfed in her chair she looks like an animated doll. I can't see her feet beneath the table, but I'd be willing to bet that they're swinging a good six inches off the floor.

In the ordinary course of my life, I don't encounter many nuns, and if I do come across one I tend to see only the habit and veil. Sitting opposite Sister María, I make a deliberate effort to look past the uniform and view her as an individual. She is thin as well as short, with high cheekbones and thick glasses that magnify her eyes into murky brown pools. She holds her hands clasped in front of her on the table as if in permanent prayer. Around one wrist she has looped a small knitted purse, and around the other she wears a simple watch with a black leather strap. When she smiles, which on first meeting is not that often, she shows a full set of even white teeth. Her skin is pale and remarkably smooth— at odds with the wiry sprigs of gray hair I can see poking out from under her veil.

I try to guess her age—somewhere between fifty and sixty. But then she tells us she came to the monastery when she was twenty-five years old; and later, when we ask, she tells us she's been here for fifty-four years. I quickly make the calculation. The woman is nearly eighty years old. Living proof of the sustaining qualities of a sheltered life spent out of the sun, and what I assume is an ordered existence that's stripped of choices and the daily anxieties of modern life. I dial back to the year she first came here. It must have been 1955 or 1956. Eisenhower was president of the

United States. The Suez Crisis was ringing the death knell of the British Empire. Stalin was dead, but Russian tanks were threatening Hungary. Mao Tse-tung had finally defeated the Nationalists. And here in Spain, General Franco was looking ahead to twenty more years of unrestrained power.

Sister María smiles when she sees my surprise. "You should meet *la Anciana*"—the old one—she says. "She's ninety-three."

"And the youngest?" I ask.

"That would be Sister Sara," twenty-seven years old, from the nearby small town of Reus. "She's been here for six years, serving her apprenticeship."

"So is she the most recent recruit?" I ask, sounding as if I'm conducting an interview rather than holding a conversation. To make matters worse, I use the word *recluta*, the only Spanish word I know for "recruit," which unfortunately implies that Sister Sara was a military conscript, frog-marched here against her will like a reluctant private, rather than coming here of her own free will.

Sister María lets this pass. "That would be Sister Elena," she says—thirty-three years old, from the village of Arbeca, which is just seven miles from here. "She's still a novice."

"So is new blood still coming into the monastery?" Another stilted question that might seem innocent, but it's loaded with the knowledge that Spanish monasteries are finding it hard to drum up applicants—understandably, a sensitive topic.

Sister María looks away. "Not right now," she says. "The women who might join us have other commitments, other work they feel they must do. But all it takes," she says more firmly, "are the shoots of belief. And then the women will come. Then God will call them and they will hear."

As for her, she says the decision to "take the veil" was never in her hands, so it was not one she had to make. I brace myself for a story to rival *Abelard and Heloise*—a tale of shame, of the kind that used to drive ill-used women into the cloister. But there's no confession, no revelation. All she says is, "I was called by the Lord so it was not up to me. I was given no choice. I *had* to be a nun."

"So did she find it hard?" I ask. "When she first joined?"

"The silence was hard," she says. "I was just a young girl."

"So you weren't allowed to speak?"

She quickly rejects this idea, saying the vows of silence that nuns supposedly take are just an out-of-date myth. Perhaps— once—there might have been vows. But now, she says, "we observe silence as much as we can, but there's nothing that mandates we cannot speak."

I'm left with the impression that gossip would be frowned upon. But if the circumstances demanded, it would be okay to shout "Fire!"

✠

Nun joke number one (not told to Sister María):

A nun enters a monastery that has a strict code of silence. "You're allowed to speak only once every ten years," the abbess tells her, "and if you speak then, you're only allowed to speak to me, and to say only two words."

After ten years of silence, the nun goes to the abbess and says, "Food bad."

Another ten years of silence go by, and the nun again goes to the abbess. "Bed hard," she says.

There's a further ten years of silence before the nun returns to the abbess for a third time. "I quit," she says.

"Well, I'm not surprised," the abbess tells her. "You've done nothing but complain ever since you came here."

✠

Sister María invites us to join one of the many services the nuns attend. "But only if you want to," she says, making it clear that there's no pressure. "It's not our job to preach or teach," she tells us. "We never try to bring other people into the Church. We don't proselytize. We don't try to commit others. We just commit ourselves. It is our job to come in to the monastery, and then to pray."

And pray the nuns do, day after day following the same routine with only a few minor adjustments:

Matins at 6:00 a.m. (aka Vigils)

Laudes at 8:00 a.m. (spelled "Lauds" in English-Latin)

Eucaristía at 8:30 a.m. (this is Mass, which is sometimes combined with another service)

Sexta at 1:00 p.m. (known as "Sext" in English-Latin)

Nona at 3:45 p.m. ("None" in English-Latin)

Vespres at 7:30 p.m. (also called "Vespers")

Completes at 9:20 p.m. (called "Completas" in Spanish; or "Compline" in English-Latin)

"Life is prayer," Sister María says, when I ask if she ever tires of this daily routine. "Prayer, contemplation, and work."

"And what about faith?" I ask. "Where does that come from? And how can someone without it manage to acquire it?"

I'm hoping for a long and considered response—perhaps even a give-and-take discussion. But Sister María is well past that stage and has distilled her ideas to a single, straightforward statement. "Faith comes from God," she says in a way that leaves no room for dialogue or doubt. "There is no other source. You cannot find faith on your own. It can come only from God."

✠

Once back in our own part of the monastery, we explore the rest of the *hospedería*. We've been told that the cells here are often full—occupied by visiting members of the nuns' families, by clergy who need a bed for the night, or by paying guests like us. But right now we're the only people here. Our cell is near one end of a long row of similar cells that ends in a small library containing a boardroom table, several stiff-backed upright chairs, and a smattering of religious tomes and magazines, mostly in Catalán. Upstairs on the third floor, there's a cupboard full of mops, buckets, and brooms, as well as a simple chapel with five rows of wooden pews set in front of a plain altar.

We have an hour to spare before Vespers—the service we plan to attend in the monastery's church—so we have time to explore the town of Vallbona de les Monges. It's a charming place with narrow winding streets and small sandstone houses, but right now it's also eerily quiet. As we climb the hill to the edge of town, we pass a scrap of newspaper discarded in the gutter. A cat prowls in a doorway. And a semaphore of garments hang on a clothes line. Other than that, there is little sign of life. We do come across two or three people—a man sawing wood in his garage, an old woman sweeping her doorstep with a hazel-stick broom, and another man inexplicably seated in a striped deck chair in the road by a car. But they're like extras in a zombie film, intended only to highlight the fact that we are the last two humans on Earth.

At the edge of town where the buildings stop and the corn-fields begin, we find a middle-aged man perched on a chair that he's tilted back to rest against the wall behind him. Above his head a neon sign flashes the word *Restaurante*. He rocks forward when he sees us, his impressive stomach, like a water-filled balloon, rolling him onto his feet.

"*Buenas tardes*," he says. "Please. You come in. You like to eat? You like good food? Then you must come in."

We look past him into the restaurant. Dozens of tables have been set with checkered cloths and knives and forks neatly lined up beside inverted glasses and folded napkins. Every one of the tables is empty. The owner presses menus into our hands and sweeps us inside. A waitress hurries towards us, and two cooks emerge from the kitchen, perhaps to see what customers look like. The owner visibly deflates when we tell him we're unable to stay as we have a date with some nuns.

"*Quizás mañana,*" I tell him—perhaps tomorrow.

We try to ease his disappointment by turning our attention to a battery of photographs that covers one wall. There must be twenty or more of them, all showing the same subject: the owner, dressed to the nines in a smart suit with collar and tie, standing to attention in the company of the king—Juan Carlos himself (or Juan Carlos Alfonso Victor María de Borbón y Borbón-Dos Sicilias, to give his full name), who has occupied the Spanish throne for some thirty-five years, ever since Franco died and democracy was restored.

The owner perks at our interest and gives us a tour. This photograph, he says, shows him standing a few feet from the king. This next one shows him behind the king, while the one beyond that has him a few inches closer to the king, but more to the left. The photograph above shows him standing with the king, but now on his right; while the one above that shows him still with the king, but with his head tilted a little to one side. The next photograph shows the owner and the king in the same positions, but now it is the king who has tilted his head. In the next photo along, we see that the king has turned to his right and is smiling as if at a private joke. And in the photograph below that, the smile has gone, but the king has moved a little to the left with the owner now a few steps behind.

"So you have met the king?" I ask.

The owner pulls himself up so he stands several inches taller. "Oh, yes," he says. "I have met the king."

"What, here?"

"Alas, no." Not in the restaurant. The king came to Vallbona de les Monges, but only to visit the royal tombs that the monastery preserves. These include the stone sarcophagi we thought were abandoned outside the church, as well as one or two graves that are inside the church. The owner was invited to attend as a guest, because, he says (straightening his shoulders), he was at the time *el alcalde*—the mayor.

"When the monastery was full, the town was alive," he tells us, "and when I was young, we had a population of more than five hundred. By the time the king came to visit, the number was still three hundred and fifty. But now,"—he shakes his head—"now we are down to one hundred and twenty. And still we are falling."

He looks wistfully around his empty restaurant. "There are no shops left in the town. No stores. Only houses. And as for the people,"—he raises both hands and puffs out his cheeks—"they all want to go, so they now disappear."

✠

We head back down the hill to the monastery and circle around the outer walls to the church. The door that was locked before now swings stiffly open when I lean a shoulder against it. I peer into the darkness and take a tentative step over the threshold, like Indiana Jones entering a burial chamber that's been sealed tight for a millennium or two.

The smell of damp is strong enough to touch, and the high stone walls are spotted with mold. They are also bare, as if they've been stripped by robbers who broke in eons ago and made off with everything shiny that wasn't screwed down. There's a simple altar at one end and a couple of tombs, presumably royal, at the other. Jesus is present, nailed on his cross, but other than him, there is no one else around. The church could seat hundreds—easily the whole town—but now it holds the two (or possibly the three) of us, along with an errant pigeon that's trapped somewhere up in the rafters. We gaze at the rows upon rows of vacant pews, then select a couple of seats near the back and settle in to wait.

At 7:30 p.m. precisely, a side door opens and the nuns file in. The door is near the far end of the church and connects directly to the cloister so the nuns can enter without being seen by—or seeing for themselves—any passersby in the outside world. With a small stab of guilt I realize I'd been hoping to witness a spectacle of some kind—a solemn waddle of nuns like penguins on the march. But the reality falls well short of my expectations. There simply aren't enough nuns to put on a show—eight, nine, ten in total—and they're all but lost in the cavernous nave of the church. There's nothing to herald their arrival, no music, in fact no sound at all except for the soft shuffle of their sandaled feet and a few coughs and sniffles brought on, no doubt, by the dank and stagnant, mildewed air.

Most of the nuns are as elderly as Sister María, with stooped figures and (where visible) wispy gray hair, but two at the back of the line are relatively young. One, wearing a white veil, must be Sister Elena, the novice that Sister María told us about. It's my understanding that she will spend several years immersed in the life of "prayer, contemplation, and work," then take her Simple Vows to become a juniorate nun. Only later will she move on to her Solemn Vows (if the community lets her, in a secret vote), which will lock her in for life. At that point, she will have to shed all of her worldly possessions by giving them to the poor, to members of her family, or to the community she is about to join.

The other young nun—pale-faced and slight—has to be Sister Sara, who has only recently taken her Simple Vows. She glides smoothly over the floor as if on well-oiled casters. One of the other more elderly nuns disappears behind the bulk of an organ, while the rest maintain their single file before breaking ranks to take their seats in the choir—four on one side and five on the other—so they're facing off across the chancel.

They thumb through their hymn books while the nun at the organ strikes a note to set the key. And then they start to sing. I'm expecting their voices to be lost in the hollow of the church, but one of the nuns—it's Sister Sara—has a magnificent voice, a stellar soprano. It's startlingly clear, a pure, heavenly sound that soars up to the vaulted roof, sweeps past the altar, and comes floating along the nave to where the two of us are sitting. I can scarcely believe it. I feel like Simon Cowell discovering Susan Boyle on *Britain's Got Talent*. It's a voice I could listen to for hours, one that deserves a much larger audience than a couple of errant sinners and a wayward pigeon.

The singing is interspersed by short prayers, readings from the Bible, and long moments of contemplative silence that allow for additional praying (or for the chance to let your mind wander and be filled with pleasant thoughts of what you might have for supper). When *la Anciana*—the old one—reads from a text, she stands at a lectern and grips its sides for support. A microphone crackles, but its amplification serves only to highlight the frailty of her voice. It is all too easy to foresee the time when the nuns fade away, one after another, until Sisters Elena and Sara are the only two left.

Half-an-hour after they entered, the nuns all stand, recite one more shared prayer, then bow their heads and take their leave. As they file out in an orderly line, they briefly pause before turning their heads towards the altar and then looking up. They wear strangely expectant expressions, as if they've all been waiting for the Number 10 bus and have seen it arrive at the same time.

✠

Back in our cell, we set up a picnic of tuna, tomatoes, bread, olives, and fruit. Until recently, El Reial Monestir offered three meals a day to its paying guests, served in the room that now functions as the *locutorium*, but now, with just ten mostly elderly resident nuns, it is no longer able to do this. I open a bottle of *tempranillo* and arrange our two chairs so we can sit and look out through the open French windows at the houses and rooftops immediately outside. During the day, swallows swooped and dived through the air, but now, in the evening, it's the turn of the bats. They fly towards us like kamikazes only to peel off at the last moment, playing chicken.

This is only our second day here, but already I've grown to like the *hospedería*. It's quiet and peaceful with an unhurried pace that's enhanced by the walls around us that have silently witnessed nearly nine hundred years of history. I can't resist running my hands along them whenever I dash through the *locutorium* in an effort to beat the light-on-a-timer. When their foundations were laid, the Second Crusade was still under way. They were three hundred years old when Gutenberg printed the first of his Bibles—and nearly five hundred years old when the *Mayflower* landed at Plymouth Rock. That gives them a sense of stability that's hard to replicate.

We sit quietly and sip our wine, watching the last rays of the sun seep through the sky and turn the roofs of the houses the color of a bruise. The Madonna and Child—pasted onto the pyramid of wood—perch on the table beside us like a couple of guests we didn't invite. Mary looks sad, and so does the infant Jesus.

Medieval artists always struggled to depict the baby Christ because they had to show that he knew his fate. His expression, therefore, could never be that of an innocent child, but had instead to be the troubled frown of a middle-aged man. The Jesus beside us is no exception. He sits in the folds of Mary's dress, looking less like a god and more like an anxious ventriloquist's dummy.

{THREE}

FOR THE NEXT FEW DAYS, WE USE OUR BASE IN EL REIAL MONESTIR de Santa María de Vallbona to explore the country around us. The nuns don't mind, we are free to come and go as we please.

On one of our forays, we visit Santa María's two sister monasteries at Poblet and Santes Creus. Both are within a thirty-mile radius, and along with the one in Vallbona, they form what's billed as *La Ruta del Cister*—the Cistercian Route. This route has no historical basis that I am aware of, but is instead the creation of an enterprising tourist board that hopes visitors to one of the monasteries will stick around long enough to see the other two as well.

On the day of our visit, we fire up the Panda and head southeast to Montblanc, a medieval town topped off with a crenellated castle, a remnant of its long and complex history; then head west towards El Reial Monestir de Santa María de Poblet—the Royal Monastery of Santa María of Poblet. Like its counterpart in Vallbona de les Monges, Poblet was founded in the second half of the twelfth century—in 1151, to be precise—when a Count Ramon Berenguer IV donated an unproductive parcel of land for its construction.

Today the monastery shows clear signs of the wealth it once enjoyed, even though it lay in ruins for much of the nineteenth century. Spain's monasteries have suffered greatly during their thousand-year-long history, but never more so than during the liberal reforms of the 1830s, which were aimed at reducing the power and wealth of the Roman Catholic Church. These reforms were inspired in part by similar moves made in France during the French Revolution. But they were also driven by good old-fashioned jealousy and greed.

In 1833 the Spanish crown fell into a tizzy because King Fernando VII, who died that year, had rescinded one of the ancient Salic laws—a sexist one that was aimed at preventing women from ruling as queens. This law had been instituted in Spain more than a century before by Philip V, a Bourbon who wanted to stop the rival Hapsburgs from regaining the crown through a female line.

For a hundred or so years, the law was unchallenged, because the rightful heirs all happened to be male. But Fernando VII had no sons, only daughters, and he wanted the elder of the two to succeed him. When he rescinded the Salic law to bring this about, he upset his younger brother, Carlos, who had been patiently waiting in the wings as the next in line to the throne. Fernando's rescission worked, however, and the daughter, Isabella, was duly installed as queen.

At the time, Isabella was still a child, so she fell under the sway of her scheming mother, who served as regent. The queen and her regent proved too liberal for many people's tastes so they found themselves opposed by a conservative bloc that included the Catholic Church. The Conservatives rallied around the frustrated Carlos, hoping to place him on the throne, and so launched what later became known as the first of the Carlist wars, which began that year—1833—and ran to 1840.

By 1835 the Liberals had run out of money, and when they cast around for a source of funds, their eyes fell on the conservative Church and its many lands and buildings.

Monasteries were closed, their assets seized and then auctioned off.

Poblet was especially hard hit by this monastic dissolution, because it had lost all support of the common people. For years the monks of Poblet had abandoned any pretense of poverty, chastity, and devotion. Many had royal connections and lived accordingly, with their own servants attending to their every need. When kings and nobles came to call, the monks joined them in lavish parties where they took full advantage of a degenerate mix of courtesans, harlots, and whores. The common citizens were naturally incensed—especially when they realized they were picking up the tab for this depravity through tithes imposed on them by the Church.

The monks of Poblet were given twenty-four hours to vacate the premises. The monastery was then looted and laid to waste. Its books were burned, its treasures stolen, its relics dispersed, and its walls torn down. For nearly one hundred years, the monastery of Poblet lay in ruins, but in the 1940s a small community of Cistercian monks moved in and slowly began to rebuild. The walls were restored, the sixteenth-century *retablo* was repaired, and so, too, were the royal tombs that had been defaced.

Today, the monastery boasts a new chapter house, library, *locutorium*, and refectory. And there is stained—rather than plain—glass in the church windows. But to my mind, the atmosphere of the place is wrong. Poblet remains a functioning religious community with thirty resident monks. Visitors can stay there (men only, please; no women). But the reconstructed walls, the new ticket office, a souvenir store, and the prominent signs saying THIS IS A UNESCO WORLD HERITAGE SITE all conspire to give the impression that Poblet has once again surrendered to mammon, catering now to bus tour groups looking to enjoy a brief "monastic experience."

Santes Creus is considerably better. It, too, was founded in the twelfth century—in 1158—and it, too, was sacked in 1835 and then later restored. But no one lives there now, and it's not possible to stay there. However, you can enjoy a superior sound-and-light show that runs nonstop in the chilly confines of the *scriptorium*—the room where the monks once illustrated their manuscripts. It tells you more than you're ever likely to want to know about monastic life in the Middle Ages. Suffice to say it was cold, dark, dismal, and short.

☩

When we return to Vallbona, we meet up with a man named Carlos Baz. He helps run the small gift shop the Cistercian nuns have set up, along with a young lady named Aida, who sports a gel-spiked hairdo, a raspy smoker's voice, and a silver nose ring through her left nostril. Carlos is more conservative. He's lightly bearded with speckled gray hair, large eyes, and an expressive face that sometimes says more than he does. When we meet him he's dressed in a short-sleeved checkered shirt, dark blue trousers, open-toed sandals, and no socks.

He offers to give us a tour of some of the off-limits parts of the monastery—ones we're not allowed to explore on our own—and leads us into the cloister, which is the oldest part of the monastery, dating from the mid-twelfth century. He points to the stonework of the columns and arches that are badly chipped and eroded. They're also heavily pitted, as if someone has scooped bits of them out with a spoon. He blames the pigeons we've seen flapping around. Their *excremento*, he says, is extremely acidic, so it eats into the stone and dissolves it. He shrugs his shoulders. But what can you do?

We stand around, gazing up at a pigeon that lurks in the vaulting above us. Its tail feathers twitch and for a moment I think we are about to experience firsthand just how acidic its *excremento* can be. The birds must puzzle the nuns, I think. Why would God have made their excrement quite so acidic when he knew they were certain to defecate on his house? Was he trying to send a message? And if so, what could it be?

As Carlos walks us around the cloister, it's clear that it's not rectangular but trapezoid in shape. Its four galleries were built throughout five centuries, so they show a variety of styles that morph one into the other—Romanesque into Gothic and then into early Renaissance. The west gallery—the one we're now in—is fourteenth century, Carlos says, but the vaulting is sixteenth century. In the south gallery—"thirteenth century, and so noticeably more austere"—he shows us some of the rooms that are no longer in use: the larder, refectory, and the *calefactorium*. This last one was the warming room—one of only three rooms in the monastery (the others being the kitchen and the infirmary) where a fire was always kept burning. A popular place, Carlos tells us, because even in the warmer months "you can feel the chill from the stones and the damp."

From the east gallery—"also thirteenth century"—we climb a short flight of steps to a common dormitory where the nuns once slept. "But no more," Carlos says. The nuns now have their own individual cells—small, but comfortable, with en suite bathrooms and central heating in winter. "But you cannot visit," he says, waggling a warning finger in our faces.

In the north gallery—"fourteenth century"—he stops to point down at the flagstones under our feet. "Nuns are buried here," he says, and we both take a reflex step back. He taps one of the stones with the toe of his sandal. "It takes many years to become a nun, but once you are in, you're expected to stay."

I happen to have read that, in Spain, you can legally have sex when you're just thirteen years old—the lowest barrier in Europe, and one that even Jerry Lee Lewis would be able to clear—but if you want to become a nun, you must wait until you're at least twenty-one. I find these minimum ages intriguing, because they say a lot about the societies that set them. Where I live in the United States, for example, you can legally drive a Hummer at the age of sixteen; and you can legally get locked and loaded with a semi-automatic AK-47 at the age of eighteen. However, if you want to push the envelope and buy a six-pack of low-alcohol beer, then you must wait three more years until you've reached the adult age of twenty-one.

"It *is* possible for a nun to leave the monastery," Carlos is saying, "but to renounce her vows, she must first get dispensation from the Holy See. So she has to be sure before she commits. She has to be certain. It's not an easy decision."

I look down at the flagstone I'm standing on. It must be a sobering experience to walk for fifty or sixty years along a pathway you know you'll one day be under. It would serve as a constant reminder of the transient nature of life—or perhaps of the fact that you'll be a long time dead. I peer around at the other stones. Some are inscribed with worn dates that record the year of death. But most bear no markings at all. Nothing to indicate a life has been lived and has come to an end. But, of course, for the nuns, life on Earth is merely the prologue—a warm-up act before they step through the portal of death and start the main event.

Carlos beckons us into the nearby chapter house—a spacious fourteenth-century room with a high rib-vaulted ceiling and a low wooden settle that runs around the perimeter. There's a *pieta*— "fifteenth century"—as well as several tombs of former abbesses who now rest beneath the stone floor. Their likenesses have been carved on the tombs in high relief, their stony faces staring sight-lessly up with suitably beatific expressions. It is here, Carlos says, that the nuns meet every day to read and discuss the Rule of St. Benedict, and to take care of any monastic business that will keep the community running smoothly.

"They lead a simple life," he tells us. "They have no personal possessions at all—*no tienen nada.*" His eyes widen as he says this, and clearly we're expected to respond in some way.

"It was Bob Dylan," I finally tell him, "who said, 'When you ain't got nothing, you got nothing to lose.'"

He nods in recognition, signifying a shared knowledge of popular lyrics. Encouraged by this, I can't help adding, "And it was Seasick Steve who said, 'I started out with nothing, and I've still got most of it left.'"

Carlos looks at me blankly. He's clearly not familiar with Seasick Steve.

He leads us into the church, through the side door the nuns used when they entered from the cloister. The monastery, he says, was plundered during the 1835 dissolution (which helps to explain the denuded appearance of its walls), but it managed to survive and is now one of the few in Spain that can claim to have been continuously occupied for eight and a half centuries. He shows us the royal tombs—"thirteenth century"—and tells us they're those of Queen Violant of Hungary and her daughter, Sanca, both of whom, in some convoluted way that's far too complex for any mortal to understand, are related to Juan Carlos, the current king, who dutifully came to visit.

"The nuns are always in need of money," Carlos says, as he leads us back into the cloister. "They get funding from the Catholic Church, and from the region of Catalonia, and from the national government in Madrid, because the monastery was declared an historic site way back in 1931. But they never have as much as they need—mainly because there aren't enough nuns to keep everything going. There used to be ninety of them once, but now with just ten—" He shakes his head and leaves the sentence hanging.

So does he think the monastery is dying?

He shrugs his shoulders. "Perhaps. Who can say?" The nuns are living as if there's a future, building new quarters for guests and thinking they might reopen the kitchen so they can serve meals in the *locutorium*. "And they're still hoping new people will join," Carlos says.

I tell him about Sister María's belief that more nuns will enter the monastery once they hear the call of God.

He tilts his head to one side. "Yes," he says slowly, "it's true that God may call. But today there is a lot of background noise. So if God calls,"—he shrugs again—"well, maybe no one will hear."

✠

On our last evening in Vallbona, we hike up the hill behind the monastery on the side of the town that's away from the main road. It's open country up here, with houses dotted around the hillside, surrounded by their own substantial yards. We turn around and look back at the town.

I've grown to like Vallbona de les Monges—just as I have warmed to *el monasterio* and its *hospedería*. I like the fact that there's just one restaurant, just one cafe, and only one place—the monastery itself—in which to stay overnight. I like the simplicity and the serenity that comes with the absence of choice. "Life is prayer," Sister María said—not a sentiment I would agree with, but one that's secure in its clarity of thought. The nuns—to my envy—have instilled their existence with a singular purpose that leaves no room for doubt and indecision.

As we head down the hill, we meet a woman near the gate of one of the houses. Like us, she is savoring the last few moments of the dying day. She enjoys living up here, she tells us, because of the space. She could not live down in the town, squashed up against the monastery walls. She likes it up here where the air moves and she's able to breathe.

She asks us where we are staying, and seems surprised when I say, "The *hospedería*."

"I didn't know you could stay in the monastery," she says, then pauses for a moment. "*¿Qué es como?*" What is it like?

It's my turn to show surprise. "You mean you've never been inside?"

She shakes her head. "Why would I do that? The monastery has nothing to do with me. Or with the town. That place is just for the nuns." She looks down at the building that forms the heart of her town. "No," she says, "it's not for me. I'd never find anything of interest there."

El Monasterio de la Virgen de Monlora

✠

La Congregación Apostólica
Marta y María

{FOUR}

THE PANDA HAS BEEN SITTING IN THE SUN FOR SEVERAL DAYS NOW, so it's hotter than a greenhouse when we open it up. Right away, we are assailed by the smell of overly ripe fruit—the peaches and melon we bought in the *supermercado* but didn't haul up to our cell. We climb in and drive away with the windows open to clear the air. The sun is high, and the sky a cobalt blue.

We pass through a few tiny hamlets—Llorenç, Maldà, and Belianes—then hit the A2 highway, where we immediately fast forward about nine hundred years. Trucks roar past us, spraying our windshield with gravel and grease. On the outskirts of Lérida, we're trapped in a snarl of roads that are not on our map. Construction delays us as we join a long line of cars and wait impatiently in their fumes. Lérida, I've read in our guidebook, is an attractive town that's rich with history, and I can see the elegant outline of a thirteenth-century cathedral that sits on a hill at its center. But here on the outskirts, we're stuck in a light industrial wasteland that's not quite ugly but is working hard to get that way. Our medieval forebears seemed able to erect harmonious edifices that were built for permanence, while the best that we can manage are tin-roofed warehouses and big-box superstores that have a ten-year life span at best.

At Zaragoza, which we reach by way of a navigational error, we restock the Panda at another Mercadona—more fruit, a can of sardines, some bread and cheese, and a large carton of cheap wine, or "plonk," as it's commonly called in Europe. In the fifteenth and sixteenth centuries, Zaragoza was one of the main centers of the Spanish Inquisition that officially ran from 1478, when it was established by papal bull, until 1834, when Spain finally passed a law to abolish it. The city then was the pious site of many an *auto da fe*, or trial of faith, which saw the Catholic Church burn alive at the stake large numbers of people it didn't like—mainly *conversos*, or Jews who had nominally converted to Christianity but were believed by the Church to be less than sincere in their newfound devotion to God. As often as not, the burnings were preceded by forced confessions, wrung out of the hapless victims by water-boarding and other tortures that in our more civilized age we know should properly be called "enhanced interrogation techniques."

✠

The second monastery we plan to stay in—El Monasterio de la Virgen de Monlora—comes into view long before we reach it. It sits in splendid isolation on top of a long, high mesa, its rectangular bulk like that of a barracks or prison outlined against the blue of the sky. It makes an ideal setting for a defensive building, since the monastery must have a commanding view of the plains that surround it. Even from a distance, it's easy to imagine a company of stout-hearted knights repelling an attack by throwing pots of boiling (extra virgin) oil onto the enemy below.

We pause at the junction where the minor road we're on crosses the east-west A125, then continue north toward the modest village of San Gil Luna. There we dogleg back in a long detour that allows us to approach Monlora from the rear. This is the only way to climb the cliffs and so breach the monastery's natural defenses. At the Río Arba de Biel, a narrow stream that flows through the town, we have a choice: ford the river or drive across it on what, from its rounded arches, looks like a Roman-era bridge. We opt for the bridge and are just able to squeeze the Panda between the stone pillars that guard each end.

As we start the long climb to the top of the mesa, we are immediately warned by a sign that the road ahead is *peligroso*— dangerous. Yet the surface is paved and here on the backside of the mesa there are no sizable cliffs we could inadvertently drive off. The danger, perhaps, lies in the fact that the road is single-track, so it would be easy at one of the many bends to hit another car coming towards us. Except that there are no other cars . . . and there haven't been for at least the past half hour.

We take a long run at the hill, the Panda's hair-dryer engine straining with the effort. I settle back and relax, happy just to dawdle. Our stay in Vallbona has slowed me down, resetting my internal clock so that I'm now on medieval time, proceeding at the pace of a horse and cart. So what if we don't arrive exactly when planned? Our destination will not have moved just because we're a few minutes late.

We circle around the mesa, steadily gaining height. On either side of the road, dry-country plants—rosemary, thyme, and sage—grow in profusion and fill the air with their heavy sweetness. When we finally reach the flat of the mesa top, we are once again heading north, with the bulk of the monastery visible at the far end of a long zipper of road that stretches ahead of us like a backcountry airstrip. A gale-force wind blows, roiling the Panda, and I notice that the trees up here are lopsided and stunted, as if they've spent their entire lives hunkered down, their backs turned into the wind and their branches streaming out like banners from only one side of their trunks.

We drive past the metal footprint of a communications tower and park under the awning of a makeshift carport. There are no other cars here, no sign of life. The monastery could be abandoned. As I climb out of the Panda, the wind tries to rip my door from its hinges. I bend low against it but still get bowled along like tumbleweed towards the monastery entrance. To my left and right, I have an eagle's-eye view over the plains. The bleached fields fade into the distance, except in the northeast where they end in the glittering snow peaks of the Pyrenees some fifty or more miles away.

Straight ahead, the monastery's façade is a solid wall relieved only by a Juliet balcony above the entrance and a few small, deep-set windows that are spaced arbitrary distances apart. It's two stories high and solid as a fortress, underlining the fact that it has been here for more than five centuries and clearly has no immediate plans to move. We push against the large door and step into a stone courtyard. The wind tries to follow us, but we lean against the door to shut it out and for the first time since we arrived we manage to stand up straight.

As we cross the courtyard, a nun steps through a door to our right and comes striding towards us. Her thick-soled sandals hit the ground with a thud and her veil billows out behind her like a pair of wings. She stops in front of us, coming breathlessly to rest like a heavy-breasted bird, and immediately unleashes a tsunami of Spanish. I can make sense of some of her words and hear her say, *Hemos estado esperando*—we have been waiting—but I'm not sure if this is part of her greeting or an admonition because we are later than we had said.

"*Venga. Venga.* Come. Come," she finally says. "I will take you to your room."

The nun is about thirty years old with plump cheeks that have been buffed to an apple-red by the incessant wind. She wears a Confederate-gray habit offset by a pale blue veil wrapped tightly over her ears and secured around the back. Like the nun in Vallbona, she can't be more than five feet tall, but what she lacks in height she makes up for in width. She reminds me of one of those life-size toys with a solid weighted base: When you try to push it over, it immediately swings upright again, still smiling.

The nun hustles us through the central cloister and stops in front of a tall iron-barred gate, which appears to form the demarcation line between the public and the private parts of the monastery. The gate is not a portcullis, but nor is it a security grille. Instead, it's a combination of the two. The nun unlocks the gate and kicks it open with one of her sandals, the hinges squeaking as the bottom bar grinds through a groove that over the centuries it has etched into the floor.

We follow her up a flight of marble stairs, then along a hallway or corridor that overlooks the square of the cloister below. Along the way we pass a flea-market assortment of mix-and-match goods—an oak settle, a tall hat-stand sprouting straw fedoras, a claw-foot table, several black plastic chairs, an orphaned *retablo* panel, a selection of ceramic bowls and jugs, and a hothouse of plants thriving out of the wind. Some of the items are clearly antique, but many would be classified as religious kitsch—pottery angels and cheap metal crosses—that you might find in a souvenir store with Made in China stamped on their bottoms.

The nun strides briskly along, bursting with a coiled energy, while we jog along behind her with our bag, passing several closed doors (one of which is marked *privado*), before opening one on the far side of the square and leading us into a canteen, which, she announces, can be our kitchen.

"You can do your cooking here if you like," she says, and waves a hand at a 1950s Westinghouse refrigerator, range, small microwave, and a tarnished toaster that looks retro but just might be original. It sits on the counter next to a rickety TV. The nun

pulls open drawers and cabinets, like a real estate agent showing a house, to reveal cutlery, plates, pots, pans (wineglasses, too,
I note), and a well-thumbed Bible. The kitchen runs the full
length of one side of the square, so there is room for half a dozen
Formica-topped tables and matching chairs. "And you can eat
here, too," she says.

She opens a few more doors—to a closet, a broom cupboard,
and what once was a larder—then leads us out of the kitchen to
the fourth side of the square, where she unlocks another small
door. And there she guides us through what I can only describe
as a wormhole.

✠

Wormholes are imaginary devices—much loved by science-fiction
writers—that are rents or tears in the curved fabric of a universe
that folds back upon itself. They are extremely useful if you're a
writer, because they allow your characters to move effortlessly and
instantly backwards and forwards through space and time. I never
expected to see one—certainly not here in Monlora—but I nonetheless pass through one when I step out of the 1950s kitchen and
into the gallery of an eighteenth-century church.

I knew there would be a church here somewhere—this is,
after all, a monastery—but I did not expect to find it just off
the kitchen. Yet here I am, standing in the gallery and staring
down the length of the nave to a Baroque altar backed by a gold-
encrusted *retablo*, which has at its center—on a pedestal flanked

by neoclassical gold columns—the blue-robed figure of a seated Virgin supporting a disproportionately small, brown-frocked Jesus, who is standing upright, precariously balanced on her knee. Both figures sport shiny gold crowns.

Behind me, in the gallery, there's a massive wooden stand, taller than I am, which can hold up to four giant books, one on each of its four giant sides. It's holding one now—an oversized tome that is open to show a couple of pages marked up in staves notated with quavers and crotchets, as well as words, in Latin, that have been written below them in a flowing, jumbo hand. It's a hymn book, centuries old, which is meant to be read from the back row of even the largest choir. And here it is, not serving any purpose that I can see, but just sitting like a long-forgotten article abandoned in an attic.

I step back through the wormhole to the kitchen with its shuddering Westinghouse refrigerator and the cafeteria-style tables and chairs. Then I look along the corridor—the fourth side of the square above the cloister. A heavy wooden banqueting table has been set up here, flanked by two rows of upholstered chairs. It could easily seat all the guests at the Last Supper as well as their uninvited girlfriends and wives. Against one wall there's an ancient deacon's bench with a red-and-gold, lacquer-painted back, and above that hangs a Buddhist *thangka* and a vacant cross.

On a side table that might have come from Sotheby's, someone has arranged a nativity scene—Mary, Joseph, the baby Jesus, two plastic angels, a cow, a goat, and a My Little Pony ass. Farther along, there's an umbrella stand wedged full of stout walking sticks and festooned with a striped parasol and several straw hats of the kind an Impressionist painter might have sported when working *en plein air*. And finally, right at the end of the corridor, I can just see an embossed-tin rendition of the *última cena*—the Last Supper.

"Your accommodation is through there," the nun is saying as she points us toward another door. "All the rooms are ready, so you can take your pick, whichever one you want. And if you need anything extra"—*si no tienen todo*—"then you'll be able to find me downstairs in the bar."

We look at each other. Did she say "in the bar"?

"It's next door to the restaurant," she tells us. Which, she adds, is run by a Romanian woman. Who used to be a gypsy.

We nod wisely. Of course. A Romanian gypsy. We really didn't need to be told.

✠

There are two rows of cells—one on the same floor as the kitchen and the other on the floor immediately below. Most of them are small. All of them are clean. A few are fitted with twin beds, but many have just a single cot. Each one is decorated with a plain wooden cross hung above a simple wooden desk and chair. Each one also has a sink for washing and a small space for hanging clothes. There are no Bibles that we can see, but presumably you can BYOB—bring your own.

Just one of the cells has an en suite bathroom. We could stay there, but instead we opt for the largest room since it has two windows and therefore more light. This means we will need to use the communal washrooms at the far end of the corridor, but since, once again, we are the only overnight guests, this is not much of a hardship. In fact, it gives each of us access to a choice of three toilets, two shower stalls, and four washbasins.

Our cell is the only one with a double bed. It also has a spare single. There are clean sheets, freshly ironed, a stack of blankets in a cupboard, and fluffy white towels that have been draped over a hook near the door. The cell's windows—screened to keep out bugs—offer expansive views over the plains. They also give us eye-level sightings of the many hawks that bank and turn in the thermals that spiral up around the mesa.

On the door of our room, there's a cutely lettered sign of the kind you'd see in a twee B&B on Martha's Vineyard. It tells us we're staying in the Abrahám room. Next to us is the Moisés room; then the Ruth room, and the Isaías room, followed in turn (as we move from the Old Testament to the New) by rooms named for Pedro el Apóstol, Juan Evangelista, Santiago Discípulo, María de Magdala, and Pablo de Tarso.

We unpack a few items and set up our small desk with some of our traveling companions—the wine, beer, olives, and tomatoes—then head downstairs in search of the nun. And the bar.

✠

Back in the 1950s, when mankind first ventured into space, there was a sharp rise in the number of people who were able to spot flying saucers and other mysterious kinds of UFOs. As the space age began, a lot of people turned their attention to the skies and understandably saw what they expected to see—an influx of aliens buzzing around the heavens like bees around an opening flower.

Two thousand years ago, Jews were convinced that the Kingdom of God was about to arrive, heralded by the appearance of a Messiah. This was not a nebulous belief, but something that Jews knew was about to occur right here and right now. The dead would then rise from their graves and, led by the Messiah, join the living in a long march to somewhere even better than the Promised Land.

Not surprisingly, large numbers of Jews jumped the gun and saw what they expected to see. Resurrections were a dime a dozen—Jesus was not the only Jew to rise from his tomb—so large parts of Judea must have looked like outtakes from George Romero's *Night of the Living Dead*.

By the time the eleventh and twelfth centuries rolled around, attention had switched to the Virgin Mary. She popped up like a Whack-a-Mole—although funnily enough only in Christian Europe. She did not show up in the Muslim world, nor in Asia or Africa. And in the Americas, she waited until the sixteenth century before putting in an appearance—by which time there were enough Christians living there with expectations strong enough to conjure her up.

These days, Mary rarely makes personal appearances, but her image often does. I well remember the time—several years ago now—when her likeness turned up on a toasted cheese sandwich that a woman named Diane Duyser grilled at her home in Florida. Ms. Duyser was about to tuck into her sandwich when she saw "this lady looking back at me." Immediately she called for her husband (as, of course, one would), and quickly they realized the image had commercial potential. In 2004 she offered it for sale on eBay and quickly accepted an offer of $28,000 from an online casino called the Golden Palace that hoped the image would generate much-needed publicity—which, of course, it did.

Here in Monlora, the Virgin showed up in 1100, right at the start of the twelfth century. She did not touch down on the mesa, but instead hovered a few feet above it. We know this because her floating apparition was seen by a priest from the nearby village of San Gil Luna who happened to be passing. No one doubted his word the way cynical people today might doubt a sighting of, say, Elvis Presley, so the mesa top became a holy place. Eventually—in the early 1500s—large amounts of money were raised, and a monastery was built to mark the spot where Mary had floated.

For the next three hundred years, El Monasterio de la Virgen de Monlora (as the monastery was called) was occupied by Franciscan friars, until they were forced out in the 1830s because of the monastic dissolution. The monastery then stood empty and abandoned until 1992 when the local municipality of San Gil Luna took it over and offered it to a revolving door of religious Orders—including the Poor Sisters of St. Clare, commonly known as the "barefoot nuns" (which is a bit of a misnomer since typically they wear open-toed sandals).

Today the Sisters have gone and the monastery is occupied by La Congregación Apóstolica Marta y María—the Apostolic Martha and María Congregation. But it is managed by an organization called La Hermandad de Nuestra Señora de Monlora—or the Brotherhood of Our Lady of Monlora. And it is now firmly in charge.

☩

We learn much of this history after we make our way to the bar—and yes, there is a fully stocked bar in this monastery—and find our nun ensconced there as promised. I'd like to report that she's perched on a bar stool bemoaning the state of the world, her veil flung to one side as she slams back shots from a bottle of sour-mash whiskey that sits on the counter in front of her. But alas, that's not the case. She is merely standing at the end of the bar comparing notes with another woman who, we learn, is the Romanian gypsy who oversees the monastery's restaurant (which we can look into through an open door).

Like the nun, the Romanian gypsy looks about thirty years old, but there the similarity ends. She is quiet, slender, and darkly exotic, with large brown eyes and a tangle of free-flowing hair. She asks if we'd like a drink. I refrain from responding, "Is the Pope Catholic?" and look over her shoulder at the rows of bottles that line the shelves behind the bar. I recognize some old friends—Beefeater gin, Bacardi rum, J&B scotch—as well as a few strangers I'd like to get to know—Torres brandy, Eristoff vodka,

Anis la Castellana—but conscious of my surroundings, I show a measure of restraint and settle for a simple glass of *tempranillo*. As the Romanian pours the wine, she tells us she's part of an influx of migrants (that included more than seven hundred thousand Romanians) who flooded into Spain on the heels of one of the recent expansions of the European Union.

We take our drinks to a table, where the nun soon joins us. I'd like to buy her a drink, but I'm not sure how she'd respond. As it is, I find the nun-in-a-bar to be a strange situation, as if she's not really a nun but is instead a Strip-O-Gram model here to disrobe on somebody's birthday. Either that or she's a visual punch line to a raunchy joke. A nun, a rabbi, and an Irishman walk into a bar . . .

She sits herself down at our table, her hands clasped neatly across her round belly. Her name, she tells us, is Sister María Rosa del Carmen, and she is not from Spain but hails instead from Guatemala. Her Order—La Congregación Apóstolica Marta y María—was founded there about thirty years ago in the town of Jalapa in Guatemala's southeast highlands. It started life with just six sisters, but now has more than three hundred working not just in Guatemala and Spain, but also in Cuba, Honduras, Venezuela, Argentina, Italy, Ethiopia, and—surprisingly— Sunni-dominated Morocco.

Sister María signed on when she was just eighteen years old. She is now thirty-three and has been based in Monlora for about three years. And yes, she likes it here very much—except that "it's very cold because of the wind. It blows all the time and there's a lot of snow, too. In winter," she says, "it snows and snows, and then nobody comes."

I look around at the empty bar and through to the empty restaurant next door, and think of the run we have of the empty rooms upstairs.

"I know," she says, "there's no one here right now. But at the weekends—and in the summer—we get very busy. People come up here to dine. And to look at the view."

The nuns are allowed to stay in the monastery courtesy of the Brotherhood, which turns out to be a group of affluent businessmen (no women) who work together for mutual gain— commercial as well as spiritual. In addition to the monastery, the Brotherhood controls the bar and the restaurant, which it operates partly for profit and partly as a roundabout way to promote the Virgin.

I order two more glasses of wine as Sister María tells us the story of the hovering Virgin and the monastery's subsequent founding. I don't know how much of this story she believes, but she recounts it in a factual manner as if she were saying that yesterday it rained or that Napoleon's armies invaded Spain in 1808. "There's a tree outside," she tells us, "which shows the place where the Virgin appeared." As if that constitutes some kind of proof.

✠

Just before dark, I step outside to the car for a bottle of wine and a few olives and cheese for our tapas. The wind still blows, but now with an extra sting, bending the bushes into ghostly, beckoning shapes. I pass a small *carrasca* tree—one I hadn't noticed before—and realize now that this is the tree that marks the spot where Mary appeared back in 1100. I stop to read the plaque that's been planted at its base: Tradition says that in this place the Virgin appeared to a priest from Luna. It has particular significance for the people of this area and for the devotees of Nuestra Senora de Monlora. Respect it. Thank you.

As I struggle with the translation (the plaque, of course, is written in Spanish), I can't help wondering what would have happened if the Virgin had appeared but there'd been no priest to serve as witness. Would she have lingered? Moved on to the next mesa? Or perhaps returned at another time?

As a general rule, when visitations like this are reported—usually by shepherds or adolescent girls—the local bishop conducts a preliminary inquiry to rule out fraud, heresy, madness, or crass commercialism on the part of the beholder. If warranted, the investigation is then passed up the chain of command to the Vatican, where it is taken over by the Congregation for the Doctrine of the Faith—an organization that's every bit as august as it sounds. Its mandate is vast, since it is the administrative body for all matters that relate to doctrine or faith throughout the entire Catholic world. As such, it is the only body that's authorized to determine if a visitation is "supernatural" and therefore deserving of a "worthy-of-belief" stamp of approval.

The Congregation has yet to rule on the reported sighting of Mary-on-the-Mesa. But it's early days. It may be nine hundred years since Mary appeared, but the Church does not like to be rushed. Its investigations of the paranormal can rumble on for a millennium or two, so no one is exactly holding their breath.

✠

On the way up to our room—or to what I've come to regard as our private, fifteen-room apartment—we see two nuns tripping down the marble stairs toward us. Both are dressed in the gray habit and flowing blue veil of the Martas y Marías. They're younger than Sister María—still in their twenties, I would guess—but they have the same solid build. They look shyly at one another as we grind open the iron-barred gate, then giggle timidly when we ask them a question.

Oh, yes, they say, they like it here in Monlora, even though they've been in Spain for only a matter of weeks.

"Better than Guatemala?" I ask.

"Oh, yes," they giggle.

The two nuns have just walked the four miles up the hill from San Gil Luna, the village we drove through on our way here. They make the journey every day—walking down to the town in the morning and walking back up at night. It takes them well over an hour each way, even using the footpaths that shortcut the hairpin bends in the road, but Martas y Marías is an open Order so it's the nuns' job to go out into the world and do good works. In San Gil Luna, there's a retirement home for Catholic priests, where the nuns cook and clean and take care of the sick.

The nuns giggle at our questions, and they giggle at our Spanish. They giggle again as they squeeze past us on the stairs, and when they make the squeak-and-grind noise of the iron-barred gate. They are still giggling as they cross the cloister, leaving us on the stairs with our olives and cheese and a brown paper bag concealing our bottle of wine.

In our kitchen, we cook up a foreigner's version of a Spanish omelet, accompanied by a side salad of white asparagus and over-ripe tomatoes. We eschew the cafeteria tables to eat at the long banqueting table outside the church. Seated in our throne-like chairs, a football field apart, we feel like royalty without the butlers. The salad dish slides between us, along with the open bottle of wine that we send gliding the length of the table in the hope that neither one of us will bowl a gutter ball.

It costs nothing to stay here in Monlora. You can, if you wish, make a contribution to the monastery's upkeep, but at some point the nuns—or more likely the Brotherhood—decided to adhere to monastic tradition and offer passing strangers like us accommodation that's free.

{FIVE}

THE NEXT MORNING WE MANEUVER THE PANDA OFF THE MESA top and drive down to the village of San Gil Luna for a kick-start shot of thick Spanish coffee. We find a cafe and push open the door. Inside, a couple of locals sit on plastic-and-chrome bar stools watching a Spanish soap on a TV that has the sound turned off. A gallery of posters hangs on the walls showing local matadors with their capes raised and hips cocked to demonstrate their machismo, alongside pictures of multi-generational soccer teams posing for their in-your-dreams victory shots. A sign above the bar encourages patrons to smoke, which clearly most of them do. The air is hazy with the acrid fog of tobacco.

We scuff through the cigarette butts and torn sachets of sugar that litter the floor to take our places at the bar. We nod at the locals, who understandably seem to find their beers and chasers a lot more interesting than us. The coffee machine roars and we order a couple of fresh-looking churros—the long, spindly dough-nuts that the Spanish like to dunk in their espressos. One patron stirs himself to ask where we are from. He's an elderly man with a dark face as furrowed as the fields he probably plows and a pale forehead that a hat has shielded from the sun, making him look as if the top part of his head once belonged to someone else and has only recently been grafted on.

I tell him we're originally from England, but we've now moved to the United States by way of Canada. He nods slowly, without expression. I could as easily have said we're originally from Mars, but now we live on the backside of the moon.

As our coffee arrives, the door of the cafe opens and a gang of workmen shuffles in—eight of them altogether, dressed in identical blue-denim overalls like trustees on a day-release from prison. All of them have a logo—the name of the utility that employs them—neatly stitched onto their breast pockets. They drag a couple of tables together, scraping the legs over the floor, and order breakfast—churros and coffee, supplemented by draft mugs of Mahou beer and half-a-dozen shots of Licor 43, which they drink as a chaser or tip into their coffees to give them extra heft. They pass tobacco around, then sit back and fire up a blaze of hand-rolled cigarettes.

The coffee is hot and strong and packs a punch that instantly jerks us awake. We order two more and another round of churros, then head uphill to the local church. It's becoming a habit, this visiting of churches, as they often prove the most interesting buildings around—and the most accessible, too. We enter through a side door to discover a nave that's awash with bouquets of lilies laced together—pew to pew—by delicate strands of muslin. Lilies, I know, are often used to symbolize virginity, but they can also serve as a stand-in for death. In this case, they're being employed for both.

"We have a wedding today," a verger tells us, as he adjusts the flowers, "and a funeral tomorrow." He shrugs. "That's the way it goes. You are born, you get married, and then you die. And the Church," he says, "is always there."

✠

Stoked up with caffeine, we decide to take the Panda out for a spin around the local towns that we've seen from our eagle's nest on the mesa—the towns of Paules, Erla, Sierra de Luna, and Las Pedrosas. Each is cut from the same general mold—a crumbling church at the center, locked up tight because of its perilous state of repair, a huddle of houses around it, and farther out a few newer buildings and a smattering of randomly parked tractors and trailers. The church tower is always home to families of storks breeding in huge nests of branches, twigs, and grasses that spill over the stonework to decorate it with untamed mounds of vegetation.

Only Las Pedrosas is different. Its church has been built on a dusty mound that sets it apart from the rest of the town, and when we climb up to see it we pass dozens of tiny houses that have been dug into the hillside. The doorways are easily reached, but the houses themselves—neglected and abandoned—are all underground, their roofs formed by the sod and grass of the hillside. I cannot imagine who would have lived here, but in the past several days I've become so imbued with monastic life that I assume the houses were once retreats, occupied by miniature, mole-like hermits.

As we walk down the other side of the mound, we come across an old man dressed in a tweedy jacket and battered hat. He sits on a bench with a walking stick firmly planted between his feet, his gnarly hands crossed and resting on the handle as if he's about to break into a Fred Astaire song-and-dance routine. He turns stiffly as we approach and gives us a long country stare. It would be rude to ignore him so I offer up a "*Buenos días*," which he returns in a way that indicates he might be open to conversation.

I ask him about the underground houses, then make the mistake of advancing my theory about miniature hermits. He cocks his head to better catch what I am saying, and for a long moment his face is blank. But then it assumes a withering look as it dawns on him that I really am the idiot I so evidently appear to be.

His accent is hard for me to comprehend, but I eventually grasp that the small buildings were not houses, but were once bodegas used by the villagers for storing the wine that they produce. The temperature inside the hillside was exactly right—not too hot, not too cold—and better yet, it was constant. The villagers still produce wine, the old man says, but now they work through a regional cooperative, so the bodegas are no longer needed.

As he explains all this, he carefully pushes himself to his feet and begins to move as if slowly and painfully climbing up an invisible staircase.

"Las Pedrosas," he says, to my continuing incomprehension, and waves his stick at the town around him.

"Yes," I say, "I know the name of the town."

He shakes his head. "No, no, no. Not Las Pedrosas. *Las pedrosas*."

And finally I get it. His invisible stair walking is a mime of treading grapes. And Las Pedrosas—or *las pedrosas*—can be roughly translated as "red feet." *Ped* for feet, and *rosa* for red. Red feet that come from tromping grapes. The old man's face cracks into a smile as we inanely grin back, and then—like him—begin stomping our feet, slowly climbing his invisible staircase and crushing invisible grapes into invisible wine.

✠

On the road back to the monastery, we meet Sister María and the two younger nuns striding down the hill toward us. They are walking three abreast, their long habits fluttering behind them like Superman capes. We stop and ask if they would like a lift. They are going down and we are going up, but we can easily take them into town. They clap their hands with excitement and squeal at the prospect of a ride in a car. But not even the tiny Panda can be turned around on such a narrow road, so we are forced to drive to the top of the mesa, make a U-turn there, and head back to where the nuns are patiently waiting, praying their rosaries.

We lean over the backseat and open the rear doors, and one by one they squeeze in. But it's like trying to stuff a ten-pound turkey into a five-pound pan. They giggle like schoolgirls on a trip to the beach, their plump faces turning pink with exertion as they squish themselves in. We have to climb out and lean our weight against the rear doors as if we're trying to close an overstuffed suitcase. Only when the nuns all breathe in together do the doors finally click into place.

We climb back into the front. The Panda has sunk under the weight and now seems to be resting on its axles.

"So what will you be doing in town?" we ask.

"We're going to visit the sick," they tell us.

"Not visiting one of the bars?"

This suggestion throws them into convulsions of laughter. *¡Qué idea!* What an idea!

"You mean, you don't drink?" we ask.

They again roar with laughter. To think they might drink!

"Or smoke?"

The Panda rocks from side to side as the nuns chortle at *that* idea.

"And I bet you don't swear either?"

They can barely contain themselves. Smoke! Drink! Swear! Whatever next! I haven't the nerve to go further down our long list of vices.

At the Río Arba de Biel, I decide to shun the bridge and go for the ford. The nuns peer out of the windows at the water sloshing against the Panda's wheels. We emerge on the other bank and head into town, the butterball nuns still squeaking and squealing as we pull into the main square. The rear doors burst open and the nuns spill out like overripe fruit, quickly regaining their dignity while straightening their veils and smoothing down their habits.

"Thank you," they say demurely, then set off three abreast to the church.

☩

We head up to the mesa, leave the Panda in the carport, and take a stroll around the outside of the monastery. The yard at the back is a tangle of long-stemmed grasses that bend and shake in the wind, their silver seed heads rattling with the tinny sound of maracas. Nearer the edge of the mesa, the wind swirls and blows, lifting the dry soil into pirouettes of dust.

There's no one here now, but as Sister María said, the monastery can become crowded. Only about one hundred people stay overnight in any given year, but the restaurant is frequently full since it has a well-deserved reputation for quality, specializing in regional foods such as *chorizo a la brasa* (spicy sausage), *cerdo* (pork), *jamón* (ham), *bacalao* (salt cod), *gambas* (shrimp), and *calamares a la romana* (fried squid). Then, too, on summer weekends the mesa top is often taken over by hordes of paragliders who leap from the cliffs to catch the thermals and soar with the hawks.

At least twice a year, the mesa is also crowded with locals who make the long trek up from San Gil Luna. On September 7, they gather to reenact the miracle of the Virgin's appearance; they don't hover above the mesa like Mary did, but instead climb to the monastery and then in procession carry her image—mounted shoulder-high on a litter—down to the church where we saw the lilies. And on May 1, they gather again for a major festival that sees fifteen-year-old boys and girls celebrate the end of their childhood and the beginning of their lives as adults.

This is a festival I've witnessed elsewhere, since it's held throughout much of the Spanish-speaking world. I initially thought it was Christian in origin, because an integral part demands that the fifteen-year-olds affirm their faith in God and make a lasting commitment to the Catholic Church. In reality, however, the festival is pagan, traceable to the Aztecs in Mexico, who celebrated the coming of age of boys—considered at fifteen old enough to be warriors—and of girls—considered at fifteen old enough to be mothers.

In the sixteenth century, when the Conquistadors reached Mexico, the two cultures—Spanish and Aztec—intermingled. Christianity was an easy sell to the Indians, who were already attuned to human sacrifice and so had no trouble absorbing the idea of nailing someone high on a cross, and the coming-of-age ritual was quickly adopted—and later adapted—by a proselytizing Church that was eager for converts and so happy to accommodate existing cultural traditions.

Looking around the mesa, I find it hard to imagine that a pagan ceremony—especially an Aztec one—would mutate into a Christian-based rite. But religions—like species—evolve. They don't begin life in a fully formed state, but morph and develop until it's hard to tell where one ends and another begins. Christianity, for example, can trace many of its precepts to Zoroastrianism, a religion that began in Persia sometime between the tenth and sixth centuries B.C. and still thrives today in certain parts of Iran. Its founder—Zoroaster—spent many years wandering in search of some kind of truth and only began to preach when he was about thirty years old. He is now credited (along with the Jews) with originating the idea of monotheism when he elevated a god called Mazda to the number one position. He further came up with the idea of theological dualism—the notion that the world is dominated by the opposing forces of Good and Evil—when he faced off Mazda, the creator of all things good, against Angra, the creator of all things evil and the forerunner of Satan.

Zoroaster also proclaimed that mankind has free will, so as we make our way through life it is up to each of us as individuals to determine if we should travel the path of Light or tread the road of Darkness. He believed, too, that each of us will at some point face a Day of Judgment when our ultimate fate will be determined. Will we be taken to a place called Hell? Or will the good we have done here on Earth qualify us to enter the everlasting Kingdom of Mazda? And he believed that all mankind will one day face a Final Day of Judgment, when the dead will rise from their graves to join the living, their bodies and souls will be reunited, and everybody will march into that everlasting kingdom if the good we have done collectively outweighs the bad. All notions that have echoes in Judaism and Islam, as well as in Christianity.

Over the centuries, Zoroaster's beliefs were modified by the Magi—a priestly caste that also came from Persia. Three of them were later drafted by Christians, who had them appear as three wise men in a Bethlehem stable, where they passed the baton of godhood onto Jesus. To Zoroastrians, the three Magi would have represented good thoughts, good words, and good deeds—the central components of their beliefs—but to the followers of Christ, the three Magi were viewed as possible stand-ins for the Holy Trinity—the Father, Son, and Holy Ghost.

As the Roman Empire expanded, new gods came to the fore—most notably, a sun god named Mithras, who also hailed from Persia and had his roots in Zoroastrianism. For a while, Mithras had to take second place to Sol, another sun god who came origi-nally from Syria; but he was able to gain the top spot when, in the third century A.D., the Emperor Diocletian made him the official god of the empire. Mithras did not last long, however. At the beginning of the fourth century—in 312 A.D.—the Emperor Constantine swept both Sol and Mithras away and proclaimed himself to be a follower of Christ. He then cemented Christianity as Rome's official religion by offering tax breaks and advancement to those who professed to believe.

Mithras and Sol faded into history, but live on in the shape of the halo—seen behind the heads of saints and other holy fig-ures—and in the celebrations of December 25—the date selected for the sun god's birthday, which was co-opted by Christians and turned over to Jesus. As for Mazda, the Zoroastrian god who got the ball rolling, he, too, faded away—only to be reincarnated in the twentieth century, first as a light bulb and then as a make of Japanese car.

All of this syncretism—the heretical merging of religions—leads me to believe that one day I may find myself reading by the light of a Holy Ghost bulb, or tooling around town in a solar-powered, 3.2-liter Jesus Christ. It also makes me think that no one religion can be any more true than another.

But perhaps it's not religion that's important—but faith.

✟

That evening, we again bump into Sister María—back from her day of work in San Gil Luna—who stops by to join us for a chat at our long banqueting table.

She has always been a believer, she says. Her parents made sure she was baptized and confirmed—and introduced to the Church as a child—so now she has no real way of saying where her faith came from or how it is maintained. However, she says, when growing up in Guatemala, there were just three possible paths that she, as a woman, was able to follow in life. She could remain single. She could marry a man. Or she could marry Jesus—or *El Señor*, as she sometimes calls him.

"I chose Jesus," she says. "And now I am married to him. I am married to *El Señor*."

As she tells us this, she toys with a ring on the wedding finger of her right hand. The ring is plain except for a small engraved cross, and clearly she's been wearing it for a long time. Her sausage-like fingers have fattened around it so now it's embedded into her flesh. I don't think she would be able to remove it even if, in an unlikely event, she tried.

She leans towards us when she talks about what Jesus has come to mean in her life. Ordinarily, Sister María has so much vigor she can barely stay in her seat, and on several occasions she lets rip with a hurricane of laughter that eventually subsides into a giggle. But when she talks about Jesus, she lowers her voice and speaks slowly and clearly as if she wants to make sure we understand his supreme importance.

Her Order, she says, has twenty-two "houses" throughout Spain, so she could have been sent almost anywhere in the country. She had no say in the matter, since she has taken vows of "obedience, poverty, and chastity," which means she goes wherever she's told. Every five years, she is allowed to return home—to visit her family in Guatemala—but she has no desire to go back and live there. She's happier here giving help to the sick and aid to the poor, and she is now learning Italian in the hope that her next assignment might be in Rome.

I point out that there's more poverty in Guatemala than there is in Spain, given that the average Spaniard is about ten times better off than the average Guatemalan.

"Yes," she says. "But there are poor people everywhere, even in Spain. So I just do as I'm told and go wherever I'm sent. I have to. I don't have any other choice. Not if I want to stay married to Jesus."

✠

Nun joke number two (could have been told to Sister María, but wasn't):

A man checks into the emergency wing of the Sister of Mercy Hospital. Before his operation a nun asks him how he plans to pay for his treatment.

"Are you covered by health insurance?" she asks.

The man painfully shakes his head. "No," he croaks.

"Well, can you pay cash?"

"I'm afraid not, Sister," he whispers. "I have no money."

"Then how about a relative—would one of them be willing to pay?"

He again manages to shake his head. "I only have the one relative. My sister. But she's a spinster nun in a convent, so she's broke like me."

"There are no spinster nuns," the man is sharply told. "They are all married to Jesus."

"Well, if that's the case," he says, "you can send the bill to my brother-in-law."

✠

On the morning of our last day, we are packing up the Panda when Sister María comes billowing out of the monastery under full sail. Like a diligent public-relations manager, she thrusts a brochure about her Order into my hand—a reminder, she says, of where we have been and who we have met. At her request, we exchange e-mails. Then she rushes back indoors.

As I reverse the Panda out of the carport, I hear a shout and look back to see her filling up the Juliet balcony above the monastery's main door. She's waving wildly, both arms swinging through the air.

"We will pray for you," she shouts. "We will pray for you. And *El Señor*—he will be with you. He will be with you in your car."

She is still waving as we head down the airstrip of a road, and the last words I hear are another blessing as it comes wafting on the wind towards us.

El Monasterio de San Salvador de Leyre

✠

Benedictine

{SIX}

MANY YEARS AGO, I READ ABOUT A STUDY OF THE GENERAL knowledge that American students possess when they first enroll in college. The authors of the study asked a sample of students a series of questions, including one that said, "What do you think the holocaust was?" Most students gave the correct answer, but one declared that the holocaust was a Jewish holiday. So he was half-right and received a passing grade.

When I was a student, I thought the holocaust was the worst crime the human race had yet committed. But now I know better. It was merely a manifestation of the worst crime, and probably not the culmination.

For two thousand years, devout Christians have systematically persecuted Jews. After all, God sent his only son to Earth and the Jews killed him, so of course they needed to be hounded, crushed, and slaughtered.

This allegation is, of course, nonsense for any number of reasons. Crucifixion was a Roman punishment, not a Jewish one; if the Jews had been solely responsible for killing Christ, then they would have had him stoned to death. Also, if God had wanted his son to die on the cross, then the Jews would have been guilty only if they'd saved him. And finally, did Jesus really want his followers to persecute Jews when he was himself Jewish, when he preached only to Jews, and when in Matthew 15:26, he apparently considered non-Jews to be "dogs"?

And yet the accusation sticks—and so, too, does the punishment, traceable to a single line in the Bible, Matthew 27:25, in which the Jews who wished to see Jesus dead are quoted as saying, "His blood be on us, and on our children." That one simple sentence was enough for those Christians who took their Bible literally to sanction the wholesale slaughter of a people. Only in 1974 did the Catholic Church concede that perhaps not all Jews were guilty of deicide; and only in 2011 did the Pope state explicitly that the Church had made a mistake when it condemned a race.

I'm reminded of all this when we stop in the small town of Sos del Rey Católico in the province of Zaragoza. Since leaving Monlora, we have been driving north and slightly west through a stratum of history that is broadly defined by the tenth, eleventh, and twelfth centuries. We passed through Sádaba, where we walked around the perimeter of a renovated castle (complete with turrets joined by crenellated ramparts), and since then we have seen so many road signs pointing us towards tenth-, eleventh-, and twelfth-century churches that we've ceased to show much interest.

This, unfortunately, is a period of history I know little about, except to say that this part of Spain—the Christian part—was then divided into small independent kingdoms that almost invariably were ruled by kings called Alphonso. By my count, there must have been close to twenty Alphonsos before the royal families—about to run out of fingers and toes—reluctantly switched to Roderick and Roland, with the occasional Ferdinand thrown in to keep everyone alert.

This surfeit of Alphonsos is often confusing, since it's almost impossible to tell them apart. But it does allow you to appear wise and informed because no matter the Spanish event that's up for discussion, you can always tug thoughtfully on your chin and say, "Hmmm, wasn't that during the reign of Alphonso?" You have an excellent chance of being right, as long as you don't assign the Alphonso a number.

The Muslims who invaded the Iberian Peninsula were nowhere near as considerate. Their names, such as Tāriq ibn-Ziyād, Abd-ar-Rahman, and Yūsuf ibn Tāshufīn, greatly complicate a study of their lives. But as if to compensate, they contrived to ensure that significant events occurred only in easy-to-recall years. They first came to Spain in 711 (a memorable date, as it employs the same digits used by the 7-Eleven convenience stores), and they finally left—or were driven out—in 1492 (another easy date to recall as it corresponds with the year that Columbus "discovered" the Americas).

Between those two bracketing dates, the Muslims scheduled other events to occur in easy-to-remember years. In 1010, for example, they created the *taifa* of Dénia, a Muslim kingdom in Spain that came into being after the collapse of the Caliphate of Córdoba, and in 1212 they lost the game-changing battle of Las Navas de Tolosa, which drove them out of central Spain. ("Hmmm," you might say, "wasn't that battle fought during the reign of Alphonso?" And, of course, you'd be right! Number VIII, if you need to keep count.)

Strangely enough, the Muslims appear to have done nothing at all in the year 1000, giving us zippo to remember in that easiest-to-recall date. But perhaps they were just following the pattern set in year one, when again nothing of note seems to have occurred—not even the birth of Jesus, which the year was supposed to mark. This pattern has been upheld during our own time, as the year 2000 is best remembered for what didn't happen rather than for what did: The Y2K millennium bug failed to materialize, and George W. Bush failed to win the US presidential election.

But that's history for you.

✠

Sos del Rey Católico would be just another one-stork town were it not for the fact that a Ferdinand was born here in 1452, and he might have been just another one-stork king had he not had the wisdom to marry Isabella in 1469 (they married young in those days in order to secure their dynasties) and begin the long process of uniting Spain under a single crown. As it is, Sos is now an important stop on a tour of Spain's history, a perfectly restored and meticulously preserved medieval town that looks exactly as I imagine it did some five or six hundred years ago.

We trudge through its narrow streets, half expecting the residents to be dressed in period costume, sitting splay-legged on wooden stools while gnawing on fire-roasted boars' legs as they swill down large tankards of ale and slap women on the backside while calling them "wenches." Instead, we encounter busloads of tourists, some eager-beaver retailers pushing local wines and chocolates, and a group of high-maintenance Spanish women with genetically modified blonde hair who must be staying in the upscale *parador* at the far end of town.

We stop for more coffee in a smoke-filled cafe, where the distracted *tabernero* never takes his eyes off the cycle race that's playing out on his TV (even while he's pouring most of our coffee into our saucers), before we track down the Palacio de Sada, the building where Ferdinand was born. There's not much to see inside, although there are a lot of signs and plaques, including one that focuses on "the Jewish problem" and Ferdinand and Isabella's "Spanish solution," which was to force all Jews either to convert to Catholicism or to leave the country.

This was a "solution" the Jews had met before, since they had first been told to convert or face expulsion in a royal decree that was issued way back in 613. Only after 711, when Muslim armies seized control of the Iberian Peninsula, did the Jews find themselves treated as equals, allowed to own land and to hold public office. Their luck did not last, however. In the twelfth century, Spanish Muslim rule switched from the easygoing Almoravides to the more fundamentalist Almohads, and the Jews once again found themselves subject to persecution.

They enjoyed a brief respite during the peak years of the Reconquista, when Christians needed skilled people to help colonize and run their newly recaptured lands and so put their anti-Semitism on hold. But then came Ferdinand and Isabella's Inquisition, followed, in 1492, by their Edict of Expulsion, which gave the Jews three months to become Christians or to go into exile. They had to wait until 1868, when a new Constitution allowed religions other than Catholicism to be openly practiced in Spain, before they were allowed back into the country, and to wait until 1968 before Ferdinand and Isabella's Edict of Expulsion was finally repealed.

When we leave the Palacio, we walk through the town to the only other building that's open to the public—the Iglesia de San Esteban. This church is eleventh century, and it shows its age in the short columns as fat and squat as sumo wrestlers' legs that support the roof, and in the small windows that keep out any light. It's as much a fortress as it is a church. We poke around the dark interior, peering into the gloom of the chapels, and then pay a small fee to descend a spiral staircase to view the frescoes in the crypt below.

Back upstairs, a priest is about to give a service. He's old and stooped, and breadstick thin, like a walking cadaver the Grim Reaper decided to throw back. Two nuns are there to assist him. They, too, are old and gray, with veils scraped back severely enough to give them face-lifts. The priest stands near the altar, wringing his hands as he intones a prayer. One of the nuns moves to the organ and strikes a few mournful notes—the start of what sounds like a wake.

As we leave the church and step into the sunshine, I look back from the open doorway and see an elderly man swathed in a coat and huddled in a pew four rows from the rear. The priest and the two nuns are playing to an audience of one.

✠

Cheering joke number three (needed to counter the gloom of the church):

"Someone's stolen my bicycle," the parishioner says.

"Never mind," the priest tells him. "Next time I give a sermon, I'll run through the list of Ten Commandments, and when I get to 'Thou shall not steal,' the thief will feel so guilty, he'll give your bike back."

The following week, the priest again encounters the parishioner. "So did my sermon work?" he asks.

"Oh, yes," the parishioner says, "even better than I thought."

"So you now have your bike?"

"I do indeed, and it was much easier than I expected. I listened to your list of Ten Commandments, and when you got to 'Thou shall not commit adultery,' I remembered where I'd left it."

✠

As we set out north on the N240, we pick up some light traffic coming out of the nearby town of Pamplona. It's the weekend —a Sunday—and large contingents of leather-clad bikers are out enjoying the sunshine and the rush of leaning low into the bends and then accelerating hard to ride out of them again. Most of the cars we pass are occupied by families, not the lone occupants I'm used to in America, and they seem cocooned in their own bubbles of festive air. Their drivers are not hunch-shouldered, speeding to close a deal before it collapses, but instead lean back with one arm out the window or draped languidly over the passenger seat beside them. We follow along at a lazy pace, then turn off the highway—just before reaching the Yesa Reservoir—to take the steep hill that leads to our third monastery, El Monasterio de San Salvador de Leyre.

Again, the Panda climbs slowly. Halfway up the hill, we pass a sign for the monastery, then two more signs for parking lots that have room for a couple of hundred cars as well as a dozen or more buses. This is not a good omen. On an earlier trip to Spain, we briefly dropped into El Monasterio de Montserrat, one of the country's better known religious centers about thirty-five miles northwest of Barcelona. We thought then we might stay overnight, since the monastery is perched in a magnificent setting, high in the mountains and embedded into the limestone rock that constitutes most of the Montserrat National Park.

On the quiet Tuesday when we arrived, we were dismayed to find hundreds of vehicles lining the approach road—the overflow from the many parking lots—plus more buses than you'd expect to see in the main bus station of Mexico City. Officials in luminous vests—with the word CONTROL stamped on their backs—tried in vain to clear the traffic. Miniature trains wound through the crowds carrying those people too old, infirm, or lazy to walk. A Disneyland funicular offered rides to the top of one of the mountains if visitors didn't like the view provided by the "Lookout of the Apostles." And prominent signs—in ten or more languages—warned visitors to KEEP AN EYE ON YOUR PROPERTY AT ALL TIMES.

Long columns of people snaked in every direction, as they lined up for information, lined up to buy tickets, and lined up to eat in the restaurants or to drink in the bars. They waited to buy religious souvenirs from the many shops and stalls. They stood in line for the museums and audiovisual displays. They got in line to use the washrooms, the banks, and the cash machines, and they lined up to get into the cathedral. They also waited to hear the boys' choir sing two short hymns, then lined up to stand on pews and lean out of the side chapels to try to catch a better view. And they waited to walk behind the altar and to touch the right hand of the iconic, twelfth-century Black Virgin, who's renowned for the numerous miracles she's been able to perform.

Leyre, fortunately, is not like that, but it can become crowded with bus tours and picnicking day-trippers. When we pull into a parking lot, we find a dozen or so cars disgorging families, but only one bus.

We draw to a stop beside it and leave the Panda in the shade of a tall, spreading pine tree. Then we scrunch our way along a gravel path that cuts through manicured gardens to the foot of the monastery's towering walls, bypassing an expansive terrace complete with fountain and a wrought-iron balustrade, which provides a viewing platform for the turquoise waters of the Yesa Reservoir, several hundred feet below.

The monastery, we know, was founded more than one thousand years ago when hermits lived in caves hollowed out of the grayish limestone of the Leyre mountains that now serve as its backdrop. In its early days, it was a wild and isolated place, which made it ideal as a refuge for kings and bishops fleeing the Muslim invaders. Then, for centuries, it offered hospitality to tired and hungry pilgrims who were walking the Camino Aragonés, one of the many routes that cross Spain from the Pyrenees to Santiago de Compostela and the sacred bones of St. James.

Like most Spanish monasteries, Leyre has changed hands several times (once Cluniac, then Cistercian, it is now Benedictine). Throughout the years, it has frequently been abandoned, restored, renovated, and added to, so its appearance today bears little resemblance to its original plans. A major restructuring took place in the sixteenth century. There was another round of rebuilding in the nineteenth century (after the monastery's third abandonment, in 1836, when it fell into ruin), and a complete restoration took place during much of the second half of the twentieth century.

We're booked into one of the older parts of the monastery—a seventeenth-century wing where the monks once slept—so I'm anticipating a stone-walled cell that's cool, dark, and dripping with history. But when we reach the main entrance, we find that this part of the monastery is so old it has turned full circle and once again become new. Not just restored, but completely rebuilt. Converted, in fact, into a modern hotel that, although sympathetically handled, is still—well, modern.

I suppose I shouldn't complain—everything looks to be chic and attractive—but nonetheless I feel let down. A modern hotel—no matter how many stars Michelin may award it—can never provide the novel experience of an ancient monastery, or the escape we're seeking from tourist Spain.

We are checked in by a young Spanish woman who is polite and charming and every bit as efficient as an American.

"*Bienvenido*," she says. "I hope you have a nice stay. And a nice day."

We walk past the restaurant and its hubbub of noisy conversation (it's bursting at the seams with a late-afternoon crowd being served by attentive, white-uniformed waiters) and take the elevator two flights up to our room. It is immaculate—but as I feared, it's also prosaic. A standard double. An upscale version of a no-surprises Holiday Inn with perhaps a few personal touches, a hint or two of European taste, and a view from the window of a neatly trimmed, well-tended lawn.

The place feels like a resort, not a *hospedería*—with trails for hikers snaking up into the mountains and water sports for boaters on the sparkling reservoir below. It's very much at odds with the contemplative life that we had expected, and while that might have been ideal under other circumstances, on a trip like this—where we're hoping for novelty—it's clear that we will need to look elsewhere. In the Romanesque church, perhaps, which we can see at the far end of the lawn. Or in the small community of Benedictine monks who, we suspect, are locked away somewhere within the monastery's other main wing.

✠

On any journey through Spain, seven o'clock in the evening should be the time when it's normal—indeed desirable—to be found propped up in a bar, a drink in one hand and tapas in the other.

But not, unfortunately, on this particular evening.

In exchange for a fee of 2.40 euros, we are handed a key to the Romanesque church we can see from our window, then we walk around the outside to let ourselves in through the main (locked) door.

The church is dark inside, with just a single shaft of light streaming through a plain glass window in the wall above the door behind us. We switch on a set of lights by inserting a slab of plastic (attached to the key ring we've paid for) into a slot on the wall, and for a moment we stand in an awed, subdued silence.

The nave of the church is divided into three, with two rows of thick columns holding up a soaring Gothic roof. It is not symmetrical. Instead, the left-hand arch at the far end is notably thinner than the one on the right. It also leans to the left while the right-hand arch leans to the right, as if the two sides of the church have had a theological spat and decided to go their separate ways. More worryingly—but not surprisingly—there is a sizable, lightning-bolt crack in the stonework between them.

We wander around the side chapels and feel the oppressive weight of the centuries that this church has absorbed. There's something daunting—even intimidating—about a man-made structure that's close to a thousand years old, something that speaks of a permanence that far outshines the short span of a human life. It forces you to connect not just with the distant past, but also with a remote future you know that you will never see. There's something daunting, too, about the sheer size of the stones and the great height of the vaulted roof, proof of the effort and toil, the physical struggle that must have gone into the church's construction. It underlines the strength of the convictions of the people who built it. This, the stones say, is intended to be a true and lasting monument to God.

The door of the church opens with a squeak, and a large party—part of a tour group—streams in behind us. And right away the atmosphere changes. We move to the front of the church and sit in one of the pews and wait as more people enter. They cross themselves and bow their heads in the direction of the altar before sliding into the rows of pews. It's seven o'clock, time for Vespers. And it appears to be a full house.

A black-robed monk enters through a side door and sets up four candles in a row on the altar. He leans forward and uses a cigarette lighter to ignite them, which for some reason I find at odds with the surroundings. It's the way he leans forward and extends the lighter that makes me think of Humphrey Bogart putting a flame to the end of Ingrid Bergman's cigarette in *Casablanca*, or of Lauren Bacall in *To Have and Have Not*, standing at the top of a flight of stairs and hoping that Bogie will light her up. There's something in the manner with which he flicks his Bic that seems a little too slick, too worldly, too hip. He should, I think, have used a match.

More lights come on, and at the far end of the church a well-aimed spotlight illuminates a delicate, gilded statue of Mary with the Christ child resting on her knee. Another monk enters and slides into position behind the church's piano-organ, his bald head rising above it like the dome of a speckled brown egg. Double doors on our right swing open and two lines of monks file in. As they enter the church, they dip their hands in a stoup of holy water, cross themselves, and bow stiffly towards the altar. Their hair is white, thin, or long ago departed, and nearly all of them wear small, round, wire-rimmed glasses of the type you'd expect to see on a group of people who spend much of their time reading indoors in poor light. Their seats creak as they take their places in the choir.

Another door opens and a monk in a bright green, embossed cloak strides in. He's pumped with energy and is clearly the leading man. He takes center stage and seats himself on an elevated throne with the statue of Mary peering over one shoulder. As he settles onto his throne, he unfurls his cloak like the wing of a giant bird so I can see that it's emblazoned with two red stripes and a row of gold crosses. Its thick, starched material gives the cloak both shape and strength, so it does not flop like a Batman cape, but instead stands as far from his body as a hooped skirt.

As the service progresses, the monks sit and stand and sing in unison like a well-rehearsed chorus line. At times, one of them breaks ranks to perform a solo or to read a verse or two from the Bible. The organ quietly plays—music to relax by, not to inspire—then gives way to a prolonged period of silence that lets the congregation shift and shuffle and cough as noisily as a concert audience during an intermission.

The monk in the green cloak then steps forward. A white-cloaked helper hands him a silver censer, which he swings back and forth as if he's a golfer ghosting his stroke. He shrouds himself in a fog of incense that's as thick as the smoke from a bonfire. When his face finally emerges, I can see that it's set in an expression of adoration. After several minutes, he hands the censer back to his helper, who swings it towards the assembled monks and then towards the congregation.

Another helper comes forward carrying a solid silver column with a wheel at the top, which looks like an expensive lollipop. He sets it on the altar and fiddles with a miniature key to unlock the wheel and swing it open like a locket. He puts a flat white disk of bread inside the wheel, and then everyone kneels. Several more minutes pass in silence before Brother Green grasps the lollipop in both hands and dramatically raises it high in the air as if it's a hard-won sporting trophy. He stares at it for several minutes more, then thrusts it at the monks behind him and then towards us. His eyes never leave the trophy, but embrace it with an intense, adoring, and committed glare. There's another long silence while everyone gazes at the wheel and the small disk of bread that's locked inside.

At some point, the bread will no doubt be consumed by the monks in a kind of cannibalism that's called theophagy, a practice adopted by the early Church to appease and attract pagan people. Other societies—ones we typically view as primitive—still consume the bodies or ashes of their dead in the hope that they will absorb the power and strength of the deceased. But Christianity, in some of its forms at least, is the only religion I know of, which not only has degraded and abused its god, but also then eats his body as well as drinks his blood.

I find this strange—and more than a little disturbing.

☩

With the service over, we duck downstairs to the crypt to finish our tour of the church. It's eleventh century, with massive pillars that support the church above—each one a fat column of roughly hewn, mellow stone. I walk among them, bent low, and find one that's had an inscription etched into its surface—Matias Salinas, which I take to be a person's name—and beneath that, in a similar hand, a date—Año 1729. At one time, this would have been viewed as graffiti, an eighteenth-century act of vandalism that fortunately was crafted before the invention of spray-from-a-can paint. But so many years have passed since the name and date were inscribed that they've now been "transubstantiated" into a valuable piece of history.

I have seen this kind of evolution before—on cliffs in Colorado, for example, where Richard Wetherill, the white discoverer of Cliff Palace in Mesa Verde, scrawled his initials in the adobe mud of Spruce House; and on the Gate of All Nations in Persepolis, Iran, where Henry Morton Stanley inscribed his name (and date) as well as that of his then-employer, the *New York Herald*. Both were acts of vandalism—now history—which people like me travel hundreds of miles to see.

Back outside in the fading daylight, we pause to admire what's left of the intricate carvings of the church's Romanesque doorway and then walk around the far side of the monastery, hoping to find another public way in. Our route, fortunately, takes us past a cafe-bar that offers tapas and churros, as well as a supporting cast of beers, wines, spirits, and liqueurs. The monastery is temporarily forgotten as we turn our attention elsewhere.

An unknown time later, feeling well fortified and ready to continue our explorations, we emerge into darkness and walk next door to a still-open *recuerdos*, or gift shop. We step inside to see a Friar Tuck clone serving behind the counter.

There are several tourists with him in the *recuerdos*, inspecting an array of gifts that most people would recoil from receiving. They shuffle along, their feet seemingly shackled together, as they stare with that glazed-eye expression that comes over people

who've spent too much time looking at Virgin Mary fridge magnets and terra-cotta armies of votive candles.

We join them at one of the displays to study the miniature
statues of Jesus, key rings with crosses, jars of honey, and snack-
pack offerings of caramelized nuts. There are also rounds of
cheese, ranging in size from hockey puck to Mack-truck tire, as
well as bottles of liqueur that I see from the label are produced
right here in the *Bodegas Leyre*—the Leyre cellars. The labels on
the cheese show a cowled figure with a tonsured head and a well-
satisfied paunch, while those on the bottles feature a group of
monks having a grand old time mixing up ingredients like ancient
alchemists about to make gold.

The monk behind the counter matches the one whose picture
graces the rounds of cheese. He is moonfaced, with thinning hair
and a contented stomach that fills out his long flowing habit. He
also wears the wire-rimmed glasses of a typical monk, which keep
sliding down his nose until he pokes them back up with a finger.

I'm tempted to buy a jar of the honey, since like the liqueurs
and the cheese it has "Leyre" written all over its label. But when
I approach the counter, I'm told by the monk that the honey is
produced elsewhere. As is the cheese. And the candles. And the
bookends, crosses, key rings, pencil sharpeners, angels, bracelets,
posters, and magnets. These items may all bear the Leyre name,
the counter monk tells me, but the regulations of the European
Union are now so complex the monastery cannot comply with
them all. So the monks just license the Leyre name, stamping
their brand on other people's products. Apart from the liqueurs,

the knickknacks and curios I see all around me might well be the output of Kmart, Target, or a sweatshop in China. But certainly, they do not come from here.

This makes me wonder if even the counter monk is real. Perhaps, I think, he's just some local who has driven up from the nearest town dressed as a monk but carrying in his pocket a business card that says he also does clowns on birthdays and a jolly Santa Claus at Christmas.

{SEVEN}

THE NEXT DAY WE MEET WITH A MAN WHO CLEARLY IS THE genuine article. He's Padre Francisco Javier Suárez Alba, the Benedictine monk who has been nominated as the public face of the Leyre monastery. He is not an easy man to see. Leyre may be the site of a modern hotel, restaurant, sizable cafe-bar, and gift shop, but—like Vallbona—it is still a cloistered community in which the monks make a conscious effort to keep themselves as removed as possible from the outside commercial world. But we persevere, determined to see what life in Leyre might be like behind the high monastery walls, and persuade the counter monk in the *recuerdos* to make the introduction.

Padre Francisco looks to be about forty-five years old and sports the regulation wire-rimmed glasses. He also has poor teeth (by American standards), thinning hair (obligatory for a monk), and traces of a mild, but corrected, harelip. He is charming and urbane, quick to establish common ground as any experienced host might do. He is also funny, with an infectious laugh that comes lightly infused with garlic.

Contrary to our expectations, he is plainly a man of the world. When he learns that for several years we lived in central London, he recounts a visit he paid to that city, mentioning Hyde Park and Big Ben and the upmarket area of Kensington where he stayed in church accommodation. We nod in recognition of these familiar landmarks, and, as he intended, immediately feel at ease with an established, ready rapport.

Padre Francisco speaks reasonable English (as well as French and Italian) but says he prefers to express himself in his native Spanish. He reads a lot, he tells us, and recently spent two years in Rome on a philosophy course "with people from all over the world." He also studies history and has a deep understanding of the Church's past, as well as a mastery of its numerous splits and schisms.

At one point during the preliminary niceties, he asks me what denomination I belong to. Reluctant to confess that I might not be a believer, I sidestep his question by telling him (truthfully) that I was raised in the Anglican tradition. This elicits a long scholarly joke that has as its punch line an oblique reference to the Duke of Alba. When Padre Francisco sees my look of incomprehension, he adds a brief explanation—"the Duke of Alba, of course, being the Spanish general who was the scourge of Protestants in sixteenth-century Netherlands"—graciously allowing me to nod and laugh in the right place.

✠

We met up with Padre Francisco in the gift shop—the one public place where selected monks and any laypeople can interact—but he soon ushers us into one of the monastery's inner rooms, the *locutorium*, where we sit at a polished wooden table in the uncomfortable, high-backed chairs that I'm beginning to think have been assigned to all Spanish monasteries as a form of penance.

The *locutorium* is elegantly proportioned with a gleaming red-tile floor, a black-beamed ceiling, and long tall windows through which I can see a well-tended garden, the terrace, and a magnificent view over the glittering waters of the Yesa Reservoir. Huge canvases of angels saving sinners hang on the walls, and in each corner of the room intimate groupings of chairs have been sociably arranged around low-slung coffee tables. What strikes me most, however, is the palpable silence—broken only by the tick-tock of an antique pendulum clock as it counts off the seconds. The *locutorium* walls must be several feet thick. And there is no hint of the damp we encountered in the equivalent room in Vallbona—a testament perhaps to the much greater wealth that Leyre evidently enjoys.

Padre Francisco places the small leather purse he has been carrying on the table in front of him, and beside it he carefully positions a Logicom mobile phone, having first fussily checked to make sure it is still switched on. A large vase of flowers has been set on the table between us. The flowers look fresh, but when I surreptitiously feel their fauve-colored petals, I find that they are fake.

The padre—"please call me Francisco"—gives us a potted history of Leyre, then tells us the monastery now belongs to the government of Navarre. As the sole owner, the government is liable for the costs of the monastery's upkeep, but under a contract that appears to have no term, it allows the monks not only to live here rent free, but also to keep the proceeds from the gift shop, the cafe-bar, hotel, and restaurant.

"We used to have a small farm, too," Francisco tells us. "We kept pigs and chickens, and they brought in some money. But now we're down to just twenty-one monks, so there aren't enough of us to keep the farm going. We just raise rabbits. Which we sometimes eat." He has, I notice, a strange mannerism that involves lightly lifting the front of his scapular and then letting it drop into place whenever he says something funny or something he thinks is outlandish. He does this now, in relation to the rabbits, when he adds, "It's important always to make the distinction between pets and food."

He worries that no new recruits are coming into the monastery, but asks rhetorically, "What can we do?" He blames materialism and the competitive desire that most people have to acquire more stuff—things they probably don't want and certainly don't need. "It's affecting not just the monastery, but the Church as a whole. People might come if they could only find God. But who is to lead them? Perhaps," he says, lifting and dropping his scapular, "we need to adopt

modern marketing techniques and launch some kind of adver-
tising campaign."

I ask Francisco to outline his typical day. It is, of course, built
around the Divine Office—or Liturgy of the Hours as it's termed
in America—that, along with Mass, has been the official set of
daily prayers mandated by the Catholic Church for centuries.
The timing of the daily routine can vary with the monastery, but
for Francisco it begins at 5:30 a.m. when he is woken in his cell by
the tolling of the bell in the church next door. He gets up, show-
ers in his small en suite bathroom, and at 6:00 joins the other
monks in the church for Matins, the first service of the day. The
monks sing psalms and listen to readings from the Bible. "In two
years," he says, "you can get through the entire book, just by reading a few verses every day."

At 6:45 he returns to his cell, where he either contemplates
or reads from "sacred texts." It is not "fun reading." At 7:30 he is
back in church for Lauds, the second service of the day, which
usually lasts for about thirty minutes. Then it's over to the refectory at 8:00 for a breakfast that is eaten in silence. "We don't
prepare it ourselves. We have someone who comes in. Usually, we
have coffee, fruit, bread and marmalade, but sometimes we'll have
a sausage or, as a treat, bacon." All the monks usually attend—
"but it's not required."

Francisco then goes back to his cell to tidy and clean it, then
heads once more the church for Terce, the third service of
the day, at 9:00. "We like to attempt a Gregorian chant, but you
need really good voices to do that well." He has been in some

monasteries, he says, where the chanting is "espantoso"—terrible. "It's particularly bad in France and Germany," he says, "and *really* bad in England." He covers his ears to mime blocking out the sound. "But don't tell anyone I said that," he adds, once again lifting and lowering his scapular, "because I'll have to deny it."

Terce—along with Misa, or Mass—lasts for an hour and is followed from 10:00 a.m. to 1:00 p.m. by a period of work, either in the gift shop or in the library. "No one goes out. No one leaves. Except in the *recuerdos*, the work is all done inside the monastery walls."

At 1:00 Francisco is again back in church, this time for Sexta—a short service that includes more psalms and another reading from the Bible. Then it's time for lunch—a more formal meal than breakfast, with the monks entering the refectory two-by-two like animals boarding Noah's Ark. They again eat in silence, but with one of their number standing at a lectern and reading out loud—usually from the Bible but sometimes from another religious or historical text. Again, he says, "it is not fun reading."

Lunch lasts for half an hour, at which point it is time for a siesta, for a stroll around the cloister, or for the chance to read one of the newspapers that are on display in *la sala de comunidad*—the common room. "We have a television in there," Francisco says, "because *la sala* is the only room in which we are permitted to speak. Officially," he says, with another laugh and a lifting and lowering of his scapular. "Most of us sleep," he adds, and again his scapular is flipped up, then floats gently down.

At 3:30 he goes back to the church for another short service—None, the fifth one of the day—followed by "shared time" that is usually filled with reading, contemplation, or prayer. At 6:00 the monks all retire to their respective cells for "private time," which is also given over to studying, reading, and prayer. Then at 7:00 they meet again in the church—this time for Vespers—where they take it in turns to play the role of Brother Green.

Dinner is at 8:00—another silent meal that's accompanied only by a further reading from the Bible, and, Francisco says, by the opportunity to sample a modest amount of the liqueurs, the *Licor de Endrinas* (20 percent alcohol) or the *Espírituoso de Hierbas* (33 percent alcohol), that the monastery produces and sells in the gift shop. The monks then assemble for a short meeting to discuss any personal issues they would like to raise, before they move to the chapter hall to consider any items that might relate to the running of the monastery and its various business affairs.

At 9:30 they return to the church for Compline—the seventh and final service of the day—then spend a few moments in private prayer in one of chapels before heading back to their cells for lights out at 10:30.

Francisco has been following this routine for twenty-one years—day in and day out, with very little variation. And he can look ahead to the same routine—again, day in and day out—for another thirty, forty, or even fifty years. Until the end of his natural life.

So does he ever have doubts, I ask, and think he might have chosen the wrong path?

He shakes his head and likens himself to a long-distance runner who has embarked on a marathon that will never end. "You may have some dark days, but becoming a monk is like entering a marriage. There are ups and downs, but you don't doubt the institution. You don't stop to question. Instead you just keep going. You have to, because it's a lifelong commitment, a lifelong effort to discover a love of God.

"The routine we follow allows us to empty our minds so we can focus only on God. We always know what we should be doing, so there is nothing to take our minds off God. There's no planning. There's no need to make a decision. This is a place to serve God. And that is what we do. That is *all* that we do. We just serve God."

⁜

Francisco is hesitant about showing us any more of the monastery than we can see from the *locutorium*, but the prospect of such an attentive audience encourages him to take me farther behind its walls.

He leads me through a double set of doors and into the cloister. It's recently been renovated and enclosed and is now in immaculate condition, with white-painted walls and a shiny wooden floor. Small statues of saints stand at regular intervals along one side. They flank high arched windows through which sunlight streams in from a small garden. Since Benedictines put a high value on manual labor, I assume the garden is one of the places the monks work when not fully engaged in prayer, but when I suggest this to Francisco he shakes his head in dismissal. "Someone comes in," he says, "and they take care of it."

He leads me past the statues and stops outside a solid oak door, gropes beneath his scapular and hauls out that ubiquitous monastic accessory—a large set of keys. He thumbs through them like a bank clerk counting out dollar bills to find the right one, then unlocks the door and pushes it open.

"The chapter room," he says.

It is pitch-black, but he flicks a switch to fill the room with the bright light of a chandelier. Almost as large as the *locutorium*, the room has a high ceiling and two rows of choir stalls that are ornately carved with what appears to be coats of arms. I stop to admire them.

"Renaissance," Francisco says, with the same casual, dismissive tone that I might adopt if I were to wave my hand at a new couch in my lounge and say, "Ikea."

He takes my arm and gently spins me around. The choir stalls, apparently, are not what we've come in here to see. I turn to face the door we came through, and find to my amazement that the wall around it is entirely taken up by a massive altarpiece that's overlaid in gold and overburdened by life-size statues of medieval saints. They are positioned above a predella with panels carved in high relief—each panel depicting what I assume is a biblical scene.

Since the altarpiece was designed to be viewed from a distance—from the back of the church it once would have graced—it appears crude and ponderous when seen up close. It is nonetheless overwhelming in both the style and skill of its workmanship. It is way too big for the room. But then I realize it's only *part* of an altarpiece. The top half is missing. Someone has taken a saw and hacked it in two, lopping off the top so the bottom half could be squeezed into this room. They've even cut a hole in the base to allow for the door—so I've just walked through a gap where a saint would have stood, as if walking through the mouth of a dragon to get on a Disneyland ride.

"It's from a nearby church," Francisco says. "The church was in ruins, so the altarpiece was spare. No one knew what to do with it, so it was offered to us in the monastery. It's Baroque," he says, an unnecessary comment given its over-the-top rendition, "which means it's the wrong style, the wrong period, for our church. So we put it in here instead."

After cutting it in two. I can't decide if this is creative recycling or a reckless act of vandalism.

He points to a few of the saints as if identifying members of a family tree. "And that's Saint Benedict," he says, pointing to a black-robed figure with a crow perched near his feet. "He's the one who founded our Order. So we're particularly fond of him."

He switches off the chandelier and marches me back into the cloister, carefully locking the door behind him. We go to the far end and stop outside another locked door. Out come the keys and we step inside.

"The refectory," he says.

It runs the full length of the cloister so it's long and narrow. Two rows of tables have been placed end-to-end with chairs to seat as many as eighty or more. But only four small tables are set with knives, forks, upturned glasses, and place mats—right down at the far end.

Could I eat here? Three times a day in silence? With the same group of people? For fifty or more years? Surely even monks must get on one another's nerves—if one of them slurps his soup, blows on his coffee, or is just too fastidious in the way he butters his bread.

When I voice these thoughts to Francisco, he says, "It's true. You may not like all of the other monks, and some of them may have foibles you just can't stand. But when you enter a community like this one, you don't try to change or improve it. You just accept it. And gradually you start to *become* the community. There's no more 'me' and 'them,' there's just 'us.' The other monks then are not just companions, not just colleagues. They truly are your brothers. And remember, it's voluntary for me to be here. I'm not in the military, I haven't been conscripted. And this monastery is not a factory or office, a place of work where I *have* to attend. So I'm here of my own free will."

He looks around at the empty places.

"Also," he says, "we may sit in the same order, so we're always next to the same people. But each day we move one place around, so we each get to sit at the head of the table. We don't want anyone to feel he's getting above the rest, and that, too, helps create our sense of community."

He carefully relocks the door as we step back into the cloister. Several times he has made a point of stressing how egalitarian the

Order is, but as we leave the refectory he holds up his keys and jingles them loudly.

"You can always tell a monk's importance by the number of keys he carries," he tells me.

Francisco carries a lot of keys.

✛

We turn left and head along the shadowed side of the cloister to stop outside the next locked door. With so few monks, and all of them presumably obeying the Ten Commandments— including the eighth, "Thou shall not steal"—I'm at a loss to understand why the monastery appears to have so much security. Francisco unlocks the door and switches on another light, ushering me into *la sala de comunidad*—the one room, he tells me again, where the monks are officially allowed to speak. It's filled with short-legged tables and leather-and-chrome chairs of the kind you might find in the first-class lounge of an airport—except that the tables and chairs have been set up in front of another altarpiece that completely fills one wall. This one, too, is clearly Baroque, with an image of God at the top, an anguished and bloody Jesus below, and beneath him several rows of statued saints looking decidedly glum and rolling their eyeballs hopefully heavenward.

Something about the altarpiece doesn't seem right—partly, I think, because of its scale in this relatively small room. But then I realize that this piece—like the one in the chapter house—isn't complete. It's just a top half—the top half of the one that was hacked in two. I want to ask more about this, but Francisco's attention is focused on a couple of dirty cups that sit on one of the short-legged tables. Or maybe it's focused on the two empty tumblers that sit by the cups and the cut-glass decanter that's half-full (or half-empty if you're a down-in-the-dumps saint on a Baroque altarpiece) of what looks to me like one of the monastery's home-made and high-proof liqueurs.

He tut-tuts in housewifely disapproval and quickly escorts me out of the room, locking the door behind him, and leading me along to the fourth and final side of the cloister. There we climb a flight of wide stone steps, palatial in scale, that are watched over by heavily framed portraits of priests, monks, friars, and yet more saints wearing long robes and even longer expressions. He turns a corner and takes me to a room immediately above the chapter house and again gropes under his scapular for his keys.

He unlocks the door and swings it open. Inside, it's not dark, just gloomy—with enough light for me to make out a hooded figure hunched over a desk and mumbling words he is reading from a large and ancient tome that lies open before him.

"The library," Francisco says, "which is where I work, classifying the various texts."

It consists of two large rooms, one an alcove of the other, and both of them lined from floor to ceiling with books. Old books, shelves and shelves of them, stretching away in every direction. Francisco nods at the other monk, who glances up but says nothing, and then he leads me around the various shelves. There are more than 6,000 books in the library, he says—all of them to do with monasticism, religion, or some other aspect of spirituality.

"So no fun reading," I say.

Some of the books are extremely old—*incunables*, Francisco calls them. Not handwritten, but rare printed books that were produced before 1500. "But only about seven or eight of them," he adds, as if every library has at least a dozen or more. "Most of the books are in Spanish, French, or Italian—not in English, because, of course, of Henry VIII and the English Reformation and his decision to renounce the authority of the Pope."

I look around with amazement. In my experience, books this old are stored in rooms that are climate-controlled. And if you want to consult one, you must first get permission from a stern librarian wearing surgical gloves, who will pat you down for any pens and pencils you might be concealing, and warn you in no uncertain terms that you are not allowed to touch the book or even as much as exhale when in its vicinity.

But here in the Leyre library, the books are vulnerable to whatever weather the province of Navarre might care to cast their way. And Francisco, rather than donning protective gloves, just plucks any book he fancies from the shelves and opens it wide. He does that now, selecting one that's leather-bound with parchment-like pages and flipping through it like a riverboat gambler rifling through a deck of cards. He almost cracks the spine as he finds the title page so he can check the date of publication: 1639.

"Not a first edition," he says, and puts it back.

Out comes another: 1722.

And so it goes, one priceless volume after another.

"But enough," he says. "I'm not sure you should really be here."

He takes me by the elbow and steers me back through the *locutorium* and outside into the sunshine. I think I'm in danger of overstaying my welcome. He's already missed Terce and may likely miss Sexta, too. But at least he's given me a tantalizing glimpse of the treasures that must lie hidden behind the walls of so many of Spain's ancient monasteries.

Ferdinand and Isabella—Los Reyes Católicos

El Real Monasterio de Santo Tomás

✠

Dominican

{EIGHT}

WE SUFFER OUR FIRST POSSIBLE GLITCH AS WE SET OFF EARLY THE next morning for Moralzarzal, a small town northwest of Madrid. We're hoping to stay in the monastery there—at El Monasterio de Monjas Cistercienses Calatravas—since it is home to a unique and ancient Order of military nuns. An oxymoron if I ever heard one. Like friendly fire, committee action, or business ethics.

The nuns, apparently, are the female counterparts of the Calatrava monks, who first banded together in the twelfth century to defend Christian Spain against the invading Muslims, and we'd been hoping to see if they matched the image we had of them clutching a lance in one hand and a Bible and mace in the other. But when we call ahead to book a cell, we are told by a fragile—and barely audible—female voice that the fifteen-room *hospedería* is "temporarily" or "perhaps indefinitely" closed.

We fall back on Plan B and phone the friars at the Carthusian-turned-Benedictine Monasterio de Santa María del Paular, located about thirty miles outside Segovia. The padre who takes our call is sorry, but the monastery adheres to a centuries-old, men-only policy—although, he adds helpfully, the monastery buildings now incorporate a Sheraton Hotel that boasts of in-room movies, a turndown service, and something called a "Sheraton Sweet Sleeper SM Bed."

The hotel clearly does accept women, but we're reluctant to explore the ramifications of the "SM Bed," so we conjure up a Plan C that requires us to push on even farther to El Real Monasterio de Santo Tomás in Ávila.

Somewhere on our journey, we cross an imaginary line that begins near Porto on the Atlantic coast, curves up towards the city of Burgos, crosses the Río Ebro, and then dips down to the Mediterranean coast just south of Barcelona. This is the line—akin to the free-slave/slave-state Mason-Dixon divide of the American Civil War—that denotes the high-tide mark of the Muslim invasion, dividing the Moor-conquered south from the Christian-held north.

Of course, back in the eighth century, when the Muslims swept into Spain like a tsunami, they did not stop neatly at this boundary, but pushed north across the Pyrenees to reach almost as far as Paris. At most, there were only about 10,000 Muslim invaders—primarily Berbers from North Africa—yet they were quickly able to take over a peninsula that, at the time, had a population of more than five million. Within a few months, they had captured Toledo—capital of the defending Visigoths—then forged on to create the western arm of an Islamic empire that was every bit as big as Rome's had been.

The Muslim advance was finally stopped by the Frankish forces of Charles Martel, who, in 732, emerged as the victor of the Battle of Tours-Poitiers, a fight that was more than a pointless bloodbath. Like the battles that Miltiades won at Marathon, Constantine won at Milvian Bridge, and Wolfe won on the Plains of Abraham, this one really did change the course of history. The Frankish victory saved Europe from Muslim domination and made Spain the only country on the continent to have a dual Christian and Islamic (and possibly Jewish) heritage.

At the time, the Muslim invasion was considered to be a cultural disaster. But with the wisdom of hindsight and the distance of several hundred years, it came to be seen as a blessing. Spain, like the rest of Europe, was then in its Dark Age. Books were rare or nonexistent, and even if available could not be read by ordinary people. The Muslims, however, were enlightened and informed, familiar, for example, with the great works of Aristotle and Ptolemy. Their greater knowledge allowed them to bring to Europe a new math from India, based on nine symbols—the numbers 1 through 9—which are a lot easier to use than the Roman ones they replaced (try multiplying XIV by IXL). They also introduced another new math called *al-jabr*, or algebra, which allowed them to tackle quadratic equations, as well as to play around with complex algorithms (thereby laying the future foundations of Microsoft, Google, and Facebook).

The Muslims also brought to Europe the art of papermaking, a skill they picked up from Chinese artisans captured during the Battle of Talas in what is now Turkestan (the small Spanish town of Játiva, in Valencia, claims to be the site of the first paper mill in Europe, set up in 1120); and they introduced a cornucopia of previously uncultivated fruits and vegetables, such as lemons, apricots, bananas, cucumbers, and eggplants. If that wasn't enough, the Muslims also brought word of the Ptolemaic map that helped Columbus to reach the Americas (and Spain to develop one of the largest empires the world has seen). And when they were finally driven out of the country, they left behind some of Europe's most striking architectural wonders, such as the Mezquita mosque-cathedral in Córdoba, the Giralda minaret in Seville, and the Alhambra palace in Granada, which now form the bedrock of Spain's off-beach tourism industry.

✠

There is no mistaking Ávila when it finally appears on the horizon. Its medieval walls, with their granite towers and perfect crenellations, undulate like a dinosaur's spine up and over the hills that surround it, tightly enclosing the churches and convents on which the city's reputation is based.

It's late as we inch through the narrow streets, then drop off the hill on which the town sits to enter another tangle of roads. Just as I'm about to turn back in search of someone to give us directions, I see a sign for El Real Monasterio de Santo Tomás—the Royal Monastery of St. Thomas—and the *residencia* where we hope to stay. A small arrow directs us around a prison-high wall to a metal gate that has been trundled ajar on well-oiled rollers.

I squeeze the Panda through the gap and park on a dirt patch of open ground, pulling to a stop beside a lopsided barrel that now serves as a garbage can. We've arrived at the monastery, but possibly we've slipped in through the back door.

The monastery is huge. The intimidating wall around it must be a mile long, as it embraces not only the monastery but also the attached *residencia*, a cathedral-size church, soccer pitch, several neglected fields, and what looks to be an abandoned orchard. The monastery-proper is a stone-walled building with a stucco façade that's been freshly painted an attractive sand-yellow. But the attached *residencia* is a cement block that must have been built with both eyes firmly on cost. It juts out from the monastery like the orphaned wing of a state penitentiary, and is clearly from a different era. The 1960s, perhaps?

We climb a short flight of steps next to a ramp that provides wheelchair access to the front door and gaze up at the cement walls that, we now see, have been sparingly seeded with rocks. The concept might have been intended to mimic the stonework of the monastery next door, but the end result would fit well into East Berlin before the Wall came down. A plaque by the entrance commemorates the architect—one Miguel Fisac—who I later discover is credited with modernizing much of Spain's architecture during the second half of the twentieth century.

We push open the main door and enter a small foyer. There's an elevator on our left, and beside that a vending machine that for a euro or two would dispense a can of Coca-Cola, a Kit Kat, or a packet of flavored *patatas fritas*. On our right is a small reception area, sealed off from the outside world by a waist-high wall and a thick sheet of glass that rises to the ceiling. No one is on duty, but a sign behind the glass invites us to ring a bell that we'll find outside by Miguel Fisac's commemorative plaque.

We press the bell, and a few minutes later a short, stubby, and generally rumpled man appears, wearing the striped blue-and-white shirt and formal dress pants of an out-of-work accountant. We fill in the registration forms he gives us—name, address, and passport numbers—and take the keys to Room 405.

"Will you be wanting lunch and dinner?" he asks.

"No," I tell him. "*Solamente desayuno.*" Just breakfast.

"As you wish." He waves his hand dismissively. He's not rude, just disinterested. It costs fifty-four euros a night, he tells us, if we want only bed and breakfast.

We bypass the stairs and ride the elevator four floors up. As we alight we peer through a metal-framed window that overlooks the rear of the building and see a vegetable garden that's a tangle of dead stalks and worm-eaten leaves, as well as a row of disused workshops and a couple of greenhouses with glass that is stained an opaque green. A road—now overgrown—winds past them to end in a short ramp that must once have given access to an underground parking lot.

We turn left and start down a long corridor. It's dark, but a switch on a timer produces just enough light to show us the way as we grope along, counting off the numbers, which have been stuck on the doors with tape. Earlier that day, when we phoned ahead to reserve a cell, we were told there were many rooms available and we could stay in the *residencia* for as long as we liked. Now I can see why. There are dozens of rooms on each of the floors, and most of them seem to be vacant. I wonder why we've been assigned to Room 405, when 101 would, I am sure, have been easier to find.

We let ourselves in and right away I am transported back to my first day in the hall of residence of the university I attended. There are twin beds, each covered with a tiger-patterned blanket, the wooden desk and chair that we've come to expect, a tiled floor, plain white walls, and a clean bathroom with a shower that, we later discover, is able to dispense an endless supply of scalding hot water. There are no pictures on the walls, no quilted quotes from the Bible, no images of Mary, and no sign of Jesus—not even as much as an empty cross.

This is a secular room, a neutral room, a dorm room in a college. There are several electrical outlets and a small printed card telling us how to get Wi-Fi. When I roll up the shutters and let in a draft of fresh air, I do not see a church but instead have a view of the Sierra de Gredos mountains dark on the horizon. This is not a cell in a Spanish monastery, even if it is attached to one. But it's still a room I think I will like since it again meets all our needs but does not try to exceed them.

✚

We walk back along the corridor with the idea of bringing up some of our supplies from the Panda, but this time we take the stairs.

On the first-floor landing, we discover a bridge that leads directly across to the main monastery building. The bridge appears to be out of bounds, so no doubt we're not meant to use it. But that, of course, only adds to its appeal.

We prowl across it, tiptoeing towards a large wooden door with a heavy metal latch. I'm about to try it, to see if the latch can be lifted, when the door is pulled open from the other side and I come face-to-face with a short, elderly man with the bronzed Spanish skin and deeply incised lines of an aging Picasso. He's wearing a dress shirt and a brown cardigan pulled down over a pair of baggy pants. Another unemployed accountant, I think.

We both take a step back in surprise, and I tell him we're staying in the *residencia*—as if that explains our presence on the bridge and why we're tiptoeing across it.

"Ah," he says, and nods his head as if in sympathy. "And so now you want to see the monastery. A good idea. Much better than the *residencia*. Come along. I'll show you around."

He ushers us through the door and into the monastery-proper.

The *residencia*, he tells us, was built in the 1960s, as we had guessed. "There's been a university here in the monastery for centuries now," he says, "and back in the sixties it was hoped that we could attract people to study religion and philosophy, our main subjects. But nobody studies them anymore. Not these days." He shrugs with a kind of resigned despair.

"The *residencia* was built to house people who never came," he says, "so it might look a little rundown. At least on the outside. Not on the inside. We've kept it up-to-date, because now it's used by cadets at the police academy and by students attending the main university in town."

He locks the door behind us and sets off at a good pace, checking his watch as he goes like the White Rabbit in *Alice in Wonderland*.

"You need to see our collections," he says. "The palace, too. And, of course, the animals."

I look sideways at him. "The animals?"

"Yes, yes," he says, somewhat impatiently, as if I'm a little slow on the uptake. "The stuffed ones we have here. If we're quick, we might just have time."

╬

He leads us down a flight of steps and hustles us along one side of what he says is the *Claustro de los Reyes*—the Cloister of the Monarchs. As he strides out, he introduces himself as Friar Blasquet, a teacher of philosophy as well as religious studies.

"How long have you been staying with us?" he asks.

"About ten minutes," I tell him, and he laughs.

"I'm eighty years old," he says, and pistons his arms to demonstrate how fit he still is, "so I've been here a little longer than that. Come along. In here."

The monastery, he says, is more than five hundred years old. It was founded by the treasurer of *los Reyes Católicos* (the Catholic Monarchs, Ferdinand and Isabella), a man by the name of Don Hernán Núñez Arnalte. "But he died before the monastery was completed, so the project fell into the hands of Tomás de

Torquemada"—the first and most notorious Grand Inquisitor of the Spanish Inquisition. "When he ran out of money and couldn't complete all the works, *los Reyes Católicos* had to step in. They provided more than enough funds to finish the job, and so turned what might have been a modest monastery into something much more grand. For one thing, they added a royal palace, which they could stay in whenever they came to visit."

The result, he says, is a monastery that is now a perfect blend of church and state, with two different names whose use is determined by the function being stressed. "Sometimes it's called 'El Real Monasterio de Santo Tomás,' but at other times it becomes the 'Palacio de los Reyes.'" It was completed, he says, in that momentous year, 1492, when Ferdinand and Isabella finally sent the last Muslims packing from Spain and also agreed to finance Columbus's first voyage of discovery across the Atlantic.

He leads us into a stateroom that was once part of the palace but is now set up as a wing of the monastery's museum.

The "monks" of Santo Tomás, he tells us, are members of the Dominican Order, so technically they should be known as "friars." "They've always been a proselytizing lot, and as friars they have never been cloistered, but instead have gone out into the secular world to spread the word of the Gospel."

Over the centuries, the Santo Tomás community has sent missionaries to all parts of the world, including those that Spain, at one time or another, has conquered or controlled. "But we've mainly focused on the Far East"—on China, Japan, Vietnam, and the Philippines (named after Philip II, husband of the English

Queen Mary and later the rejected suitor and staunch enemy of the English Queen Elizabeth I, as well as the instigator of the Spanish Armada).

"China was always a focus for us," Friar Blasquet says. "We've been sending missionaries there since the sixteenth century."

He escorts us through the rooms of the former palace, now a museum. The rooms are strung out in a row like boxcars on a train, each one filled with display case after display case of priceless objects that over the centuries the monastery has received in exchange for delivering the word of God. Rarely do the objects reflect the religion the friars were spreading; instead, they celebrate the cultures of the countries in which the friars were preaching.

There are Buddhist vases, gods, and figurines, interspersed with Japanese prints, tapestries, and double-sided screens. There are whole rooms given over to plates, cups, opium pipes, and bamboo mouth organs. We see ornate jewelry boxes, incense burners, several more Buddhist gods, a sixteen-armed Bodhisattva, a dozen or more sets of ivory tusks, a carved ivory Christ from the Philippines, open trays of old coins, an abacus, a selection of string and woodwind instruments, a set of gongs, still more Buddhist gods, a miniature palanquin, a small city of model Japanese houses, many more plates and cups, and an armory of medieval swords and halberds. They all pass in a blur as Friar Blasquet hurries us along.

Many of the pieces are eighteenth and nineteenth century, he tells us, but a few are notably older. He stops beside one—a bronze prayer bell, Buddhist, which dates from the fifth century B.C. "It's our oldest piece," he says, before moving us quickly on.

He leads the way into another cloister—the *Claustro del Silencio,* or Cloister of Silence, pausing briefly to point out a frieze of stone reliefs of arrows, yokes, and other symbols of the Catholic Monarchs. Then he doubles back into another room that's one floor up but still part of the old palace. This room is the length of a football field, with an ornate ceiling of carved, painted wood. At one time the royal court would have assembled here, he tells us, but now the room is filled with period furniture and displays of black-lacquered Chinese screens inlaid with scenes in mother-of-pearl.

He marches us in one door and out another, then down another flight of stairs, which he takes two at a time.

"Are you sure you're eighty years old?" I ask him.

He laughs. "Well, not yet. I was exaggerating. I won't be eighty until next month."

He stops in front of another display case to point out the monastery's extensive collection of porcelain plates. Each one is hand painted with delicate—yet vibrant—images of Jesus shown in biblical settings. Beginning in the sixteenth century, Friar Blasquet tells us, missionaries in China—not just the Dominican friars from Santo Tomás, but other missionaries, too: Franciscans, Augustinians, and Jesuits—encouraged the production of plates like these. The plates, with their stylized images of Christ, were excellent ways of spreading the word of the Christian god.

"These plates are all nineteenth century," Friar Blasquet says. "They're exquisite, don't you think? Just look at the detail."

Like anyone else, I've come across many different depictions of Christ, each of which has been designed to impress a particular audience. All of us warm to images of gods that look the way that we do, and not like a threatening "foreigner." So in Western Europe, Jesus is often portrayed as a blue-eyed blond with straight, shoulder-length hair; while in Ethiopia and other parts of Africa, he's miraculously black with African features and a full, Jimi Hendrix 'fro; and in Peru and Bolivia, he's frequently shown as an Andean Indian who, for his Last Supper, tucks into a spit-roasted guinea pig—a delicacy the locals would accept as the only dish fit for a god.

Here, on the porcelain plates, Jesus is shown on his cross, addressing a large crowd, and crossing the Sea of Galilee in a storm-tossed boat. But on every plate, he is a Chinese Jesus— with sloping eyes, a drooping Fu Manchu moustache, and long thick black hair that he's tied into a topknot. So it's a Chinese Jesus being crucified by Chinese soldiers while three Chinese Marys look on. It's a Chinese Jesus giving the Sermon on the Mount to a Chinese multitude. And it's a Chinese Jesus addressing a Chinese band of Chinese disciples.

There's even a Chinese Mary rocking a Chinese baby in her Chinese arms and a Chinese angel telling the Chinese Virgin she's about to have a Chinese baby. And when Jesus is being questioned by a group of Chinese Pharisees, he's shown with his palms raised like a kung-fu master who's about to cleave a stack of Chinese Torahs with just his bare hands.

✠

Friar Blasquet leads us down a stone flight of stairs and outside to
yet another cloister—the *Claustro del Noviciado*, the Cloister of
the Novitiate—which, unlike the other two, is overgrown and
neglected with a defunct and capped well in its center.

"This is the oldest part of the monastery," he tells us, as he
climbs a different set of stone steps and ducks through a door to
emerge into the raised choir-gallery of the monastery's massive
church. We're one floor up, so we're able to look down the full
length of the nave, but the best view is afforded by two protruding
areas—one on either side—that hang over the nave like boxes in
an opera house.

"That," says Friar Blasquet, pointing to one of the boxes, "is
where Ferdinand sat during the services he attended. And over
there"—he indicates the other box—"is where Isabella would
have been seated."

I like to get my history by physically linking to influential figures from the past, so I carefully stand on Ferdinand's marks, then
move across to plant my feet where Isabella's would have been.
Unexpectedly, I find I am looking straight out at the altar rather
than peering down on the top of it.

"The altar was raised," Friar Blasquet says. "Normally, it
would have been set on the same level as the congregation, but it
was raised one floor up to give the monarchs a better view."

He points to the *retablo*, which is crowded with panels depicting events from the lives of saints, including, of course, the life of

St. Thomas. To me, the saints are semi-mythical figures set in fictional or fantastic scenes, but to Friar Blasquet they are real people experiencing important moments in their lives. He introduces them one by one as if they're contemporaries of his with edifying stories to tell, then points to the stonework that surrounds us here in the gallery.

There are plenty of reliefs of arrows and yokes that we can now identify as symbols of the Catholic Monarchs (the yokes marking the union of the Aragon and Castile crowns, and the arrows commemorating the many battles waged against their Muslim foes). But there are also rows and rows of knobbly bumps that, Friar Blasquet says, are not just patterns in the stonework, but rather carefully rendered pomegranates—the symbol, he tells us, for the city of Granada and the English translation of its name.

"When the Catholic monarchs captured Granada, they completed the eight-hundred-year-long Reconquista, so the pomegranate became not just an independent symbol for the city, but it was also adopted by the king and queen, who incorporated it into their Coat of Arms.

"Of course," he continues, "this part of the church was completed several years before Granada fell, which means the Catholic monarchs were not shy about anticipating their victory. It would," he adds, "have been an embarrassment for the church if *los Reyes Católicos* had lost their struggle."

He checks his watch again and then hurries us downstairs into the nave. He pauses near the raised tomb of Don Juan, the only son of *los Reyes Católicos*, then shows us the spot where Santa

Teresa—Ávila's world-famous nun and founder of the Barefoot Carmelites—used to kneel when taking confession.

"She had a lot of her visions in this church," he says.

Finally, he bundles us into the room next door—the sacristy. "This is the room where Torquemada was buried. He was a Dominican friar as well as Isabella's confessor, so he turned the Santo Tomás monastery into not just his base but also the headquarters of the Inquisition. When he died in 1498, he was buried right here in this room." He points to one corner, now innocently occupied by a table, and I move towards it—so I can stand on the great torturer's grave.

"But he's not here now," Friar Blasquet says. "His tomb was raided in 1832 and his bones were taken away and burned."

For a brief moment, I feel overwhelmed. Catholic monarchs upstairs, Santa Teresa next door, and Torquemada here in the sacristy. But Friar Blasquet is again on the move, determined to complete his tour.

"Come on," he says, "we just have time to look at the animals."

He sets off at his customary trot. We follow along in his wake into a dark, windowless room where he positions us close to the center, as if we're playing a game of blind man's bluff and we're the two dupes wearing the blindfolds. We wait in confusion for a moment—until he throws a switch and the room fills with a blaze of light.

We're standing in the center of a vast menagerie of animals—all of them stuffed. There are rows and rows of dead animals. Birds, too. Stuck on the walls, nailed to the ceiling, and suspended in space. We turn around. There are more animals behind us, in glass cages that stretch in rows as far as we can see. Crocodiles, turtles, and lizards are frozen in place on the walls as if they've been caught in the act. There's even a walrus draped over the top of the door we just walked through.

It's a Noah's ark in here. There are swordfish, piranhas, geese, ducks, a capybara or two, several small hedgehogs, a family of guinea pigs, a few more lizards, a wolf, some rabbits, stoats, newts, a black bear rearing up on its hind legs, storks, kingfishers, an excess of snakes of varying sizes, an alligator, a roaring lion with glass-marble eyes, another crocodile, some lemurs, macaques, a couple of squirrels, mice, a horn-billed bird that's now extinct, more fish, and a wide selection of gossamer-winged bats.

It would be a surprise to find a collection like this packed into a natural history museum in London, Paris, or New York. So what are they doing here, in a fifteenth-century monastery-palace?

"Come on," Friar Blasquet says. "Time's up, I'm afraid. I'm expected elsewhere." He switches off the lights and once again plunges us into darkness.

{NINE}

THE NEXT MORNING WE FOLLOW THE SIGNS FOR THE COMEDOR AND present ourselves for breakfast in the old part of the monastery. We push at a small door that's made of frosted glass framed by a wrought-iron grille and scrape it open. We know we're in the dining hall, because there's a large painting on the wall to our right that's a knockoff of "The Last Supper." It must have been purchased by an affluent, arrogant family, because there's a puffed-up noble sitting in Jesus's chair and a small group of corseted women in large hats who are mingling with the men standing in for the disciples.

The dining hall seems small at first, since the painting on our right is close enough to touch, and we could reach the wall straight ahead in five long strides. But as we push at the door and swing it further open, we see to our left that the *comedor* runs at least the length of two of the monastery's cloisters. Tiger Woods could not hit a drive that would reach to the other end. The hall is a par three—maybe even a par four. The French court from Versailles could fit in here, and in fact there are two long rows of tables and chairs that stretch into the distance, arranged as if for a state banquet or for the wedding of the two most popular people on the planet. At the far end I can just make out another table that has been set at right angles to the two long rows, so we start towards it, our heels ringing on the tiled floor.

After what seems like an hour, we pass a small balcony set high on the long wall to our right. It's from here that a friar would have read passages from the Bible to the rows and rows of his peers dining in mandatory silence at the tables below. There would have been hundreds of them then; but now there's just us. We draw breath and keep on going, passing another significant landmark—a solitary clock that twice a day shows the correct time—until finally we reach a table set with wicker baskets of bread, as well as dishes of butter and jars of jam, plus a stainless-steel urn that dispenses institutional coffee as thick as molasses. We help ourselves, then studiously debate which of the hundreds of empty chairs we should grace with our backsides.

Ten minutes later, two other people enter the hall and start the long march towards us. They, too, serve themselves with bread and coffee, then sit down about forty places away. More people dribble in until there are about twenty of us. The others are all younger than we are—students, it seems, who, like us, are staying in the *residencia*. They come in yawning, with tousled hair and T-shirts they've just pulled on, or more likely have slept in. A few are still in their pajamas.

"So do you like staying here?" we ask a young couple who sit at our table.

"Well, the *residencia* has a laundry room," one of them says.

"And there are a couple of ping-pong tables," the other one tells us, "as well as a wide-screen TV."

"On which we can watch Real Madrid."

"And of course, there's Wi-Fi."

"Even in the elevator," the first one says.

And what about the monastery, we ask. What do they think of that?

They look at us blankly. Monastery? *What* monastery? And we all go back to our coffees.

A friar enters through a side door and begins to wipe off the tables. Like Friar Blasquet he's wearing a dress shirt and baggy pants. I ask him how many friars now live in the monastery.

"About twenty," he says. "Some are teachers, some are just resting, but mostly they're retired." They have, he tells us, all served overseas, and now they have come home to die. He does not express this quite so bluntly, but that—clearly—is what he means. "There's a hospital nearby to care for them. When the time comes, that is. And since they've worked hard all their lives, they deserve a little reward."

I ask him about the university that used to be here—the one that taught philosophy and religious studies.

He looks wistful. "It was right here in the monastery. The *residencia* was full then. And so was this *comedor*. But times change," he adds, "and the world has moved on."

He shakes his head.

"Have you seen the animals?" he suddenly asks.

Oh, yes, we tell him; we've seen the animals.

"They were brought here sometime in the 1880s," he says. "No one seems to know where they came from. Nor how they got here. But for much of the nineteenth century, the university offered a lot of courses in natural history. So it brought in the animals to show to the students. Now," he says, "no one has any use for them. But no one knows where they should go. If we only knew how they got here, we'd be able to send the whole lot back."

He's silent for a moment. "Perhaps one day," he says, "someone will decide. But for now, well—they just sit in their cases or hang off the walls."

✠

Later that day, we take a more leisurely stroll through the monastery and the accompanying palace. The rooms are now open to the public so there are a few other people milling around, as well as a number of friars who like to mingle with the visitors and relate their life stories. We meet one who's dressed in the full-length white robe and black cloak of the Dominican Order—offset, in his case, by a pair of sharp-looking sunglasses.

I ask him if he, too, worked in the Far East. No, he says, in Venezuela, where he lived for close to twenty-five years. Since we've recently returned from a trip to that country, I ask him where he was based.

"Three places," he says, and begins to list them off. "Trujillo was one," he says. But then his voice trails off and a look of irritation crosses his face as he realizes he can't remember the other two. His mind, he says, has started to play tricks, giving him a prolonged senior moment.

I ask him how old he is, and he invites me to guess. I think he could be the wrong side of ninety, but since anyone who wants his age to be guessed must think he looks young for his years, I pitch my answer low and say, "Eighty."

He's clearly disappointed. "I'm seventy-eight," he says. So I tell him I meant to say "seventy" but confused the numbers when I expressed them in Spanish.

In spite of my backtracking, I think I may have spoiled his day.

✠

We walk through the various rooms and into the sacristy, then stop near the door of the church where stone steps lead to the gallery on the floor above. I'm surprised to see a smoldering cigarette balanced on the bottom stair, a curl of smoke rising from its tip like a genie coming out of a lamp. I'm wondering what it is doing there when the door of the church is thrown open and a young woman—about eighteen years old—steps out, grabs the cigarette, takes a quick hit, stubs the cigarette out on the stairs, then dashes back through the door and into the church. She is wearing, I notice, a white, off-the-shoulder T-shirt and skin-tight jeans that are tucked into a pair of spike-heeled boots. Not a common sight in a monastery, I think. So I follow her in through the door.

The church is full and a service is about to begin. We slip into a pew a few feet from the spot where Santa Teresa had her visions of angels and Jesus. Nearby, a white-robed friar sits in a confessional, waiting for customers while flipping through what looks like a magazine. Near the front of the church, three other friars stand in a row by the altar like the Father, Son, and Holy Ghost.

There are several minutes of silence, during which the congregation tries to get comfortable in the upright pews, and then a band strikes up. I had been expecting an organ, but when I crane my neck to one side, I see a chapel where a group of musicians is formed in a circle. There are about ten of them, all in their late teens or early twenties—three with steel guitars, one on drums, cymbals, and tambourine, and another who's hitting the ivories of an electronic keyboard. The rest—including the girl with the boots—are singers in what looks like an all-female backup group.

At first their music is bright, bland, and cheerful, very much middle-of-the-road—the kind of music that Belgium might sponsor in the Eurovision Song Contest. But then the keyboard player kicks up the tempo, the guitars start strumming, and the drummer beats out a rhythm so hard he breaks into a sweat. I find myself tapping my foot on a hassock. This is more like it, I think; this will put bums on seats.

I look around at the other members of the congregation. Almost all of them are women. Middle-aged, solid, and respectable. Short, too—born in the days of Franco, when Spaniards lacked food as well as human rights—and dressed in a lot of grays and browns. They sit immobile, staring stoically forward, with not a single coiffured head bobbing in time with the music.

In front of the altar, the three friars stand equally stony-faced, sentry-still, staring back at their flock with tight disapproving expressions. The rock-beat band may have been aimed at the young, but it's clearly in danger of driving away the regular audience who've come here for Jesus.

The music stops and a woman enters the pulpit to read from the Bible. I'm surprised by this, to say the least. A woman? What is *she* doing here? To diehard traditionalists, this service must be moving from bad to worse, since the Church has recently proclaimed that ordained women belong in the same sinful slot as its pedophile priests.

The band starts up again, this time playing the kind of folk music that Peter, Paul and Mary made popular. A few minutes later, the backup singers break into a happy-clappy rendition of Bob Dylan's *Blowin' in the Wind*. I'm humming along, still tapping my feet, and wondering what Santa Teresa would have made of it all.

✠

When the service ends, we stream out of the main door of the church along with the rest of the congregation and make our way to the nearest bar. Since the Royal Monastery of Saint Thomas is located close to the center of town, it gives easy access to any number of bars, cafes, and restaurants. While we wait for our coffees, a woman arrives wearing the respectable uniform of the congregation. She could, like us, have come straight from the church.

She bellies up to the bar beside us, plants her feet about three feet apart, plumps her purse on the counter, and orders a take-out tapas from the selection of glass-covered trays in front of her. Fried kale leaves, fried eggplant, and a refried mix of pre-fried eggs and fried potato that's wilting under a glistening topcoat of oil. As she waits for her order, she fires up a cigarette and orders a San Miguel on draft, which she downs like a miner after an eight-hour shift at the coal face.

When she leaves, I call over the barman and ask him to identify one of the tapas that's been puzzling me. I think it might be some kind of potato, which has been battered and curled. But no, it's—

"Pork rinds," the man says.

"And this one?" I ask, pointing to the next tray along, which is full of rust-red slices of possible meat.

"*Morcilla*," he says. A kind of sausage. "It's made from pigs' blood."

"And these?" Crispy tidbits that are strangely hairy.

"*Oreja de cerdo*," he says.

I draw a blank on that one, and am forced to look up the term in my dictionary.

"Pigs' ears?" I ask.

"*Sí, sí*. Pigs' ears," he says.

"But they still have hairs on them."

He shrugs. "Of course. But they are only short ones." He lights a cigarette and inhales deeply. "We serve a lot of pigs in here," he says.

I'm not sure how to respond to this ambiguous remark, but I happen to know that serving pig became popular in Spain as a way of rooting out closet Muslims and Jews; if they refused to eat pork, they weren't Christian so clearly deserved to be burned at the stake.

"You serve a lot of pigs," I say, "but not too many Muslims or Jews?"

He shrugs again. *"Como les quieren."* It's up to them.

✠

One reason we're out and about in Ávila is that we're eager to see the severed finger that Santa Teresa left behind when—in 1582, at the age of sixty-seven—she finally departed this Earth.

To me, Santa Teresa will always be best known for the starring role she plays in Bernini's famous work *The Ecstasy of St. Teresa,* which was commissioned by, and still can be seen in, the Santa María della Vittoria church in Rome. In his statue, Bernini certainly conveyed the bliss that Teresa is reputed to have experienced. In fact, so effective is his portrayal that many observers have claimed, somewhat provocatively, that the ecstasy he has Teresa enjoying is so intense that it must stem from physical orgasm rather than spiritual delight. But that, I suspect, is an interpretation the Church would dispute.

Either way, the ecstasy that Teresa felt, rather than the euphoria Bernini depicts, came as a result of her many visions. "I saw an angel near me," she writes in her autobiography, *The Life of Saint Teresa by Herself,* "on my left side, in bodily form. He was not tall, but short, marvelously beautiful, with a face that shone as though he were one of the highest angels, who seem to be all of fire: they must be those whom we call seraphim. I saw in his hands a long golden spear, and at the point of the iron, there seemed to be a little fire. This I thought he thrust several times into my heart, and that it penetrated to my entrails. When he drew out the spear, he seemed to be drawing my entrails with it, leaving me all on fire with a wondrous love for God. The pain was so great that it caused me to utter several moans. And yet so exceeding sweet is this greatest of pains that it is impossible to desire to be rid of it; or for the soul to be content with less than God."

By themselves, visions like these—even if painful—are not sufficient to turn you into a saint. Just to be a contender, you must either die for your faith and thus be a martyr or you must lead a life of "heroic virtue" that incorporates justice, temperance, and moral prudence. You must also be able to withstand the stringent vetting of many committees, including the Vatican's Congregation for the Causes of Saints.

This Congregation, if nothing else, provides a lot of jobs. It consists of an administrative body comprising a prefect, secretary, under-secretary, and a supporting cast of twenty-two other officials. It also has thirty-four members—cardinals, archbishops, and bishops; five Relators (not Realtors), who ensure that the would-be saints' papers are in order; and eighty-three Consultors, who stand ready to chip in—and vote—with their five-cents' worth of specialist opinions.

To get past the Congregation, you must—in accordance with rules first laid down in the tenth century—perform a posthumous miracle that is seen to result from your direct intercession (martyrs get a free pass on this one). A single miracle won't transform you into a full saint, but it will get you to first base—meaning you'll be beatified as a kind of saint-in-waiting. To move up to full sainthood and be canonized, you need to perform a second posthumous miracle that's at least as striking as the first. That might seem like an insurmountable challenge, but until Pope John Paul II changed the rules in the 1983 Apostolic Constitution, you needed to perform double that number of posthumous miracles.

Pope John Paul streamlined the process in other important ways, too, and perhaps as a result, beatified and canonized more saints than all the other Popes combined (he has since been fast-tracked himself in the most rapid ascension on record, and is moving speedily towards full sainthood, having reached beatification a mere six years after his death). There are now more than 10,000 saints—many of whom have been conscripted to serve as Patron Saints of a cause, a country, or a mere occupation. If you ever join their ranks, you might end up rubbing shoulders with St. George, the Patron Saint of England; St. Francis, the Patron Saint of Animals; or St. Cecelia, the Patron Saint of Music, Musicians, and Poets. You could also meet up with St. Adrian, the Patron Saint of Arms Dealers; St. Gertrude of Nivelles, the Patron Saint of Cats; or St. Fiacre, who some see as the Patron Saint of Those Unfortunates Who Suffer from Hemorrhoids and Sexually Transmitted Diseases.

Under the current Pope, the Catholic Church is hoping to cast a Patron Saint of the Internet, who will presumably help legitimate programmers write concise code while thwarting the efforts of spammers, phishers, and Wikileakers. If you think you might be in the running, be warned that the current front runner is St. Isidore of Seville—a seventh-century data buff and philosopher who took on the task of writing the *Etymologie*, the world's first encyclopedia.

As for Santa Teresa, she is the Patron Saint of Those Who Suffer from Headaches, and—more importantly—she's also a Doctor of Prayer. In this latter role, she is one of an extremely select group of just thirty-three saints (of whom only three are women) who are deemed by the Church to be überholy. Santa Teresa reached these heights by writing extensively—and influentially—on the esoteric topic of orthodox Catholic doctrine. During her long lifetime, she turned out dozens of books on how to lead a meaningful and prayerful life, as well as poems, letters, and that autobiography. Some four hundred years after her death, many of her books are still in print and available in bookstores and online. *The Way of Perfection*, for example, remains a perennial best-seller. Amazon sells it for about ten dollars in paperback; the Kindle download is significantly cheaper.

✝

As you might expect, Teresa's finger is kept on display in the Convento Santa Teresa de Jesús, the convent that was built in her name on the site of the house in which she was born in 1515. To get there, we walk through the narrow streets of Ávila, but en route we're unable to resist a brief detour to explore the city walls for which the town is rightfully renowned.

The walls were originally constructed by the Romans way back in the third century B.C. They later fell into ruin but were rebuilt—in the eleventh century—by Muslim prisoners taken captive by Christians during the course of the Reconquista. ("Hmm," you might say, "wasn't Ávila retaken during the reign of Alphonso?" And once again, you'd be right! It was number VI if you're still keeping score.) More recently, the walls have been completely restored, so they are now in pristine condition.

For a couple of euros, we're allowed to climb one of their many towers and walk along the battlements, peering through the crenellations at the twelfth-century cathedral—the oldest Gothic cathedral in Spain—and at the houses that huddle up against it as if for warmth. A smell of garlic wafts up from the restaurants below as we set out to circumnavigate the town. Halfway around we are stopped by a large plaque that tells us the walls were rebuilt by Muslims and Christians working peacefully together with a helping hand from the Jews. This, surely, is a clear-cut case of City Hall trying to be politically correct.

It's true that Muslims and Christians frequently lived side by side with Jews, who for reasons of self-preservation, quietly supported whichever party happened to have the upper hand. But that's because the Reconquista was never at heart a battle of faith. Like most struggles that are supposedly waged over moral issues or philosophical beliefs, the Reconquista was primarily concerned with power and wealth—which in those days meant land. Religion was just a convenient way of dividing the "us" from the "them."

Many Arabs were Christians, and significant numbers of Christians adopted Islam and turned themselves into Muslims. Also, young men on both sides of the religious divide were willing to work as mercenaries—a recognized profession—so were answerable only to those who paid them. Christians fought on the side of Muslims, and Muslims fought on the side of Christians.

Furthermore, the two sides often found it cheaper if they lived harmoniously together with one of them paying a none-too-onerous tribute to the other. Only if one faction saw a chance for advancement—or if the other felt the tribute had become too harsh—did the two sides rediscover their religious convictions and start the struggle anew.

✠

Teresa's finger, when we track it down, is not in the Convento as such, but is instead in a gift shop next door. This seems appropriate, since religious relics have long been linked to a Church wheeze intended to exploit their commercial rather than their spiritual potential. At the Second Council of Nicaea in 787, it was declared that every church should have its own relic, so it's hardly surprising that large numbers of tibias, femurs, and skulls suddenly came on the market, along with Last Supper tables, thorns that were part of Jesus's crown, snippets of the Virgin's hair, and even a tumbler or two of her breast milk. At times it seemed that everywhere you looked, there was a tangible link to God. Some kind of body part or token that could be paraded in front of a congregation and so attract a large and paying crowd—the most popular being the Holy Foreskin, of which there may have been as many as eighteen or twenty.

With so many relics available, there was a danger that interest in them might begin to wane, so in 1563, through its Council of Trent, the Church decreed that the faithful must venerate the relics of saints and other holy types, because "through these, many benefits are bestowed by God on men." The Church was all too aware of the obvious potential for deceit and corruption—splinters of wood could be turned into priceless objects if they were labeled "part of His cross," as could rusty nails if the oxidized iron could be sold as "a stain of His blood"—and strongly advised that the veneration of relics should not be exploited for "filthy lucre." But it made no attempt to take its own warning to heart.

In Rome, the Vatican attracted hundreds of thousands of paying pilgrims when it exhibited what it said was a likeness of Jesus—the so-called Veronica—and in Paris, Notre Dame did the same when it put on display a crown of thorns, a sliver of wood, and one of those rusty nails that was supposedly used to crucify Christ. These relics still draw huge crowds today, when they are trotted out for the faithful on the first Friday of every month, on every Friday during Lent, and on Good Friday from ten o'clock in the morning to five o'clock in the afternoon.

As for the Holy Foreskin, the official one, sanctioned by the Vatican, was regularly put on display until 1900, when the Church censoriously decided it might be an embarrassment and so ruled that anyone who mentioned it—or even wrote about it in a book like this one—faced the threat of excommunication.

✠

We push open the door of the gift shop and step inside. There are no other customers, but the man behind the counter is busy arranging some rosaries and barely gives us a glance. We look around at the merchandise—plaster angels, plastic crosses, stacks of votive candles, embossed cups, imprinted bookmarks, several racks of postcards, and some fridge magnets of Mary. But no holy finger.

I approach the counter and ask the man if we're in the right place.

"*Claro*," he says. Of course.

He leads us through the store to a room at the back, which has been set up as a kind of shrine. He stands respectfully back as we examine the relics that are on display. A piece of fabric that came from one of the habits Santa Teresa wore. The sole of one of her sandals (a questionable relic for someone who founded an Order of barefoot nuns). And a stick, or cane, which she leaned on during the final few years of her life.

"And this," the man says, "is her *disciplina*"—showing us a thin flagellation cord—"which she used on herself to better identify with the sufferings of Christ."

We study this *disciplina* for a moment, then move on to the next display case, where we find her rosary beads, the crucifix she carried whenever she left home to set up a new monastery, and a large wooden cross that, a small inscription says, was made from a beam of the house in which she was born.

"And the finger?" I ask.

"Over here," the man says, and beckons us towards another display case, where we see the finger, on show, inside a silver reliquary. The finger rests in a kind of thimble and points straight up into the air. It's unnaturally long, a peculiar brown in color, and is offset by an inexpensive gold ring that rests on one of the knuckles.

"When any saint died," the man tells us, "the Church allowed parts of the body to be cut off so they could be exhibited for the benefit of the faithful."

Santa Teresa, he says, lost not just the finger that we can see here, but also the rest of her right hand, her whole right arm, her right foot, her left eye, a portion of her jaw, and her heart. He does not know where these various body parts are now. "We just have the finger."

As for the rest of her—the bit that was left over—it was returned by papal order to the town of Alba del Tormes in the province of Salamanca. "That's the town where Santa Teresa died," the man says, "so that's the place where most of her is buried."

I lean forward to study the finger more closely. I'm hoping for a revelation—to experience an inner transformation like Saul on the road to Damascus. But to me it remains just a finger.

"The nail," I tell the man, "it's badly in need of a trim." It's all I can think of to say.

El Monasterio de la
Purísima Concepción y San José

✠

Trinitarian

{TEN}

WHEN WE LEAVE ÁVILA, WE FIRST CIRCLE MADRID AND THEN enter the region of Castile-La Mancha, set on a high flat plain scoured by winds that are fierce and relentless. This is Cervantes country, and the locals here are not about to let us forget it. Everywhere we look, we are confronted by a skinny, effete Don Quixote sitting astride his naggish horse and dragging in his wake his paunchy and dim-witted sidekick, Sancho, who has to make do with a mule.

The pair can be found on every street corner and in the center of every square. Their profiles appear on every road sign and grace the lintels of every bar and restaurant door. Their images are emblazoned on every plate, mug, and T-shirt that we see in every store. They're also embroidered on every curtain in every house we pass. And when we order coffee in a cafe, well, there they are again—imprinted on the front and back of every tiny packet of sugar. It's impossible to avoid them. Turn another corner, and there they are again.

Cervantes country also means windmills. Hundreds of them, decorating every rise that in this part of Spain—near the southern end of the Spanish *meseta*—passes for a hill. In their heyday, the windmills pumped water and they ground flour. They also turned electrical generators—just as their modern-day equivalents do on the many wind farms that can be seen dotted across Spain. The windmills here, however, are now redundant. Their white-washed, cylindrical bodies support fretted wooden sails that have been tied down and firmly anchored to the ground so they can no longer turn in creaking lazy circles. That makes them photogenic—and for some reason wildly romantic. When we drive up to a cluster of them, we come across a bride and groom posing for their wedding pictures, both leaning into the wind like a couple of drunken sailors, with the bride clinging onto her train to stop it from filling like a main sail and blowing her halfway around the world like Dorothy on her way to Oz.

Several years ago, I made a resolution to read *Don Quixote*, since it is often cited as one of the hundred-best novels ever written, and since Cervantes's descendants and heirs have sold almost as many copies as McDonalds has sold sesame-seed buns. But when I tracked down a recent edition at my local library, I only managed to get about ten pages in before I keeled over with boredom. I could not tolerate the marathon sentences, nor could I identify with the "Idle Reader" Cervantes addresses in his Prologue.

Reading the book was, I'm afraid, quickly relegated to the bottom half of my long list of "things to do after I am dead."

✠

The wind is blowing up a storm when we drive into the town of El Toboso in search of our next monastery. That might be why the streets are deserted. Or perhaps we're just witnessing the effects of *urbanites*—a perennial disease of Castile-La Mancha, which forces residents to tear up their agricultural roots and head for a major city, usually Madrid. Either way, it would seem that everyone has left—and the last person out has vacuumed the streets. They are pristine clean with not so much as a cigarette butt to sully the gutters. The only sign of life is Don Quixote, who remains on guard, frozen in sculpted iron in the town's main square, down on one knee as he courts Dulcinea, the fictitious love of his life who (in Cervantes's imagination) hails from here.

The third time we circle back to this pair, we realize that once again we are hopelessly lost in a maze of Spanish village streets that must surely have been laid out with the malicious intent of confusing strangers. We're about to seek help by knocking on the door of one of the shuttered cottages when we spot an elderly man with a walking stick shuffling painfully towards us. I wind down my window and ask him if he can direct us to the monastery that we know is somewhere here in the town.

"Which one?" he says. "Clarissas or Trinitarians?"

"Trinitarians, please."

El Toboso is not a large town—just two thousand inhabitants if we're to believe our guidebook rather than the evidence of our own eyes—yet it supports two working monasteries, a sixteenth-century parish church (dedicated to St. Anthony), several museums (including one devoted to Cervantes and two to Dulcinea), and a good selection of cafes, bars, and restaurants that are now all closed. But at least it's a town in which it's easy to park—a rare attribute in modern Spain.

We follow the directions the elderly man gives us and pull to a stop in the shadow of the walls of our destination, El Monasterio de la Purísima Concepción y San José. It's immediately clear that the nuns who live here are cloistered. This is a building that has turned its back on the world. The walls that rise above us are made of warm sandstone, but they look solid and seemingly impregnable—broken only by pigeon-hole-size windows that are heavily barred and grilled.

We search for a way in and find the double doors of a church, both of them locked up tight. Nearby, a much smaller door, set below ground level and guarded by a black-iron gate, is also secured by a bolt set into the stone. More concerning, as far as our reservation for a cell is concerned, there's a hand-written note attached to the gate, which says, *Estamos de Retiro Espiritual; No Tenemos Visitas*. We are a spiritual retreat and do not accept visitors.

We double back, following the walls of the monastery in the other direction to discover another set of huge doors. They also are locked, but one of them incorporates a smaller door, inset like a cat flap, which is open a crack. A breach in the monastery's security. We push it open as far as we can, then stoop low and step blindly into the darkness beyond.

✠

In our experience, stepping into a monastery is often like stepping into a black hole. Just to do so requires a modicum of faith. Many monastic "foyers" are completely enclosed, and therefore naturally dark. This one is no exception. It takes us several moments of groping around before our eyes adjust, but when they do we see that we're in an entrance hall with a lofted ceiling and a stone-pebbled floor that centuries of feet have buffed to a shine.

The walls up to head-height are patterned with flagstones, then whitewashed up to the roof. Straight ahead are five doors—all in a row, like the stage set for a French farce. Each of the doors has a small sign beside it—neatly printed in an "olde worlde" font—which hints at the function of the room beyond. We fumble our way to the door marked *torno* since that's the only one that's open, and step into an even darker space the size of a walk-in closet. On the wall ahead, we can just make out a date—1660—that has been chiseled into the stone, perhaps by a disgruntled novice marking the occasion of her incarceration.

Halfway up the wall to our right a cupboard door is slightly ajar. I pry it open and peer in to find myself looking into what seems to be the inside of a barrel. There's a circular wooden turntable at the bottom, a matching one at the top, and the two are joined by solid vertical planks of wood like the sections of an orange. There are also two vertical barriers that divide the barrel into four, so I can see into only one quarter. When I push on one of the barriers, the whole contraption begins to revolve like a lazy

Susan in a kitchen cupboard. I'm not sure why the lazy Susan is here, but there's a buzzer on the wall beside it, so I press that. And wait. We hear the echo of feet on the other side of the barrel, followed a few moments later by a muffled voice that's heavy with suspicion.

"Yes? What do you want?"

"Tenemos una reservación," I say. We have a reservation.

This claim is met by a long silence.

"¿Una reservación?"

"Yes. To stay in the monastery."

There's another long silence. To fill the gap, I put the letter of confirmation that we received onto the lower turntable and give the lazy Susan a spin. The *torno*—which I've finally figured the device must be called—completes a revolution, whisking my letter away but returning it to me within seconds. I've clearly underrated the *torno*'s engineering. I try again, giving the *torno* a half-turn so the letter is delivered at a manageable speed to the owner of the voice on the other side of the cupboard.

A rustling of paper ensues, along with several minutes of whispering.

"There are two of you?" the voice finally says.

"Yes."

"You've come from America?"

"Yes."

Another long pause. Then the *torno* rotates and our letter reappears.

"Then wait. Please."

We step out of the closet and stand in front of the French-farce doors, waiting to see which one will open. It's the middle door that finally does, and an elderly nun steps forward, dressed in a white cardigan that she's pulled on over a white habit, and a black veil fixed over a headband that tames every last wisp of hair. Her habit is plain except for a prominent cross—blue vertical and red horizontal—stitched across her chest. This marks the nun as a Trinitarian, but also shows off the embroidery for which the nuns here are renowned. In one hand, she carries the set of keys on a jailer's ring that I've come to expect. In the other, she wields a large wooden-handled screwdriver.

The nun is typically short and wide, and moves towards us with the splay-footed waddling walk of a wind-up toy. She introduces herself as Sister María—the name that almost every nun seems to have adopted—and says, somewhat unnecessarily, that this is a closed Order. As a result, she is not able to leave the building—nor to let us inside—so to get us to our room she must ask us to walk around the monastery walls to the double doors of the church, while she will follow an interior route that takes her through the cloister.

We do as we are told, braving the cold wind, and wait by the church doors. The nun is meant to meet us here, but when she appears she does so by opening the much smaller door that is belowground, protected by the black-iron gate. She remains on the other side of the gate with one arm pushed through the bars, beckoning us forward with a crooked finger.

"In there?" I ask.

"*Sí, sí. Pase. Pase.* In here."

I look at the gate and the thick door that's open behind it. To go through there would be to enter a dungeon, and with anyone else I might have refused. But I can't see an elderly nun—even one armed with a screwdriver—luring us into a trap, so we duck our heads and once again step into darkness.

✛

The iron gate turns out to be just the monastery's first line of defense—put there to guard the solid wooden door behind it, which the nun is holding open for us.

"This is the way you must come in," she says. "And you must always keep the door locked. The gate, too. When you come in and when you go out, you must keep everything locked. We have many valuable possessions, so you must keep both the door and the gate locked. Is that clear?"

"We need to keep them locked?"

"Yes. At all times. They both must be locked."

She takes a key from her jailer's ring and shows us how to lock the gate when we go out. This is not as simple as it might sound, because the key can only be fitted into the lock from the inside. Whenever we go out, she tells us, we must reach an arm through the bars of the gate and put the key in the keyhole *sólo a tientas*— just by feel or touch.

"You must also secure the door, especially at night," she says, and again shows us how this is done. The door has more locks and bolts than a ground-floor apartment in downtown Detroit. "You must secure it. Here. Here. Here. And here."

She tries to swing the door shut behind us, but it's too heavy for her to manage. She leans her full weight against it, but she has no success until I reach over her head and surreptitiously lend her a hand.

We follow her across a tiled floor, dip low under a couple of arches, then walk past a disused well and clump up a long flight of stone steps, hunched over to avoid banging our heads against the ceiling. (This is not a problem for Sister María.) At the first landing she unlocks another wooden door and we follow her into a large room with a hardwood floor and a twelve-foot ceiling.

"This is for you," she says.

We look around. The room is furnished with one single bed, a glass-topped table, and a wooden stool. Nothing else, unless we count the poster of Jesus and the row of portraits of nuns and other religious types gazing up at the ceiling with rapt expressions of yearning and joy.

"Also in here," the nun says.

We follow her into an adjoining room where there's a wardrobe and another bed—this one a double—and then into the third room of our suite, a small but functional bathroom with washbasin, shower stall, and toilet.

"It can get cold at night," she says unnecessarily, "because of the wind. But there are extra blankets in the bottom of the wardrobe along with some spare towels."

This is good news, because the room, to us, already feels Arctic cold. Sister María turns a tap on the radiator that runs along the length of one wall and it gurgles and clanks with promise, but noticeably fails to throw out any heat. "It can take a while for the water to flow," she tells us, "because it has a long way to come. But it will get here. Eventually," she adds, and then unexpectedly drops to her knees. I think for a moment she's about to pray, but instead she attacks the radiator with the long-handled screwdriver, wielding it adroitly to undo a valve. "You have to release the trapped air," she says. "You have to let it bleed out. Also," she adds, "you have to learn the virtue of patience."

When she struggles back to her feet, I ask her how long she has been here. Fifty years, she says. Like most of the other nuns.

"It's hard for us to keep the monastery going. There's always cleaning and a lot of maintenance, too. It was easier before. There were twenty-four of us when I first came here, but now we're down to just eight."

I feel I should offer to help in some way. But Sister María seems more of a handyman than I'll ever be.

☩

After she leaves, we climb farther up the stone steps outside our suite. On the top landing we go into a meeting room that's furnished with a long boardroom table covered with a primrose-yellow cloth that has white flowers embroidered along its hem. It's flanked by a dozen or more straight-backed chairs with upholstered velveteen seats, giving the room the ambience of a nineteenth-century dining hall rather than a seventeenth-century monastic boardroom.

Next door—also off the landing—is a chapel with neat rows of pews that could seat a congregation much larger than it's ever likely to see. It's almost warm in here, thanks perhaps to some portable heaters along one wall or to the long-life votive candles that flicker away near the altar.

The carved figure of a black Jesus hangs in one corner, leaning into the chapel like the figurehead on the prow of a ship. He's wearing his post-trial purple robe—which for some reason is liberally sprinkled with sparkling sequins more suited to *Dancing with the Stars* than to his imminent crucifixion—as well as a crown of thorns, an ill-fitting wig, and an understandably anguished expression.

The wall he is facing is taken up by a pair of lattice grilles that overlook the nave of the monastery's church, one floor below. If a public service is held in the church, the cloistered nuns can sit up here and watch the proceedings through the grilles, able to see without being seen.

We sit for a moment and feel the heavy weight of the silence that envelops us, then grope our way along a gloomy corridor that leads from the landing to five tiny cells—rooms that other visitors might stay in, if they have not been blessed with our suite. Each cell contains a single bed and a table and chair, but no window. Just a framed sheet of frosted glass that can be swung open to let in a feeble light from the corridor.

There's a creepy, death-row feel to the cells, and I'm not sure I could sleep in one and still manage to pass for sane in the morning.

✠

That evening, we sneak out of the monastery—carefully locking the door and the iron-barred gate behind us. The wind is still fierce and the streets are still empty.

As a small town—and a conservative one at that—El Toboso is always going to be quiet. But since it often fills with tourists following the *Ruta de Quixote* (who come here to visit the Casa Dulcinea and the Museo Cervantes) and with rich *madrileños* (who keep as weekend retreats many of the now-vacant white-washed cottages we pass), we're hoping for at least some pulse of life. As it is, we see one decrepit car trundling along a deserted street and two rickety codgers shuffling into the town's *centro comunitario*, or community center.

We walk through the main square and drop in at the parish church to watch Saint James killing Moors as he gallops his charger above the altar. Three streets farther on a neon sign flashes *restaurante-bar* and we finally discover where everyone is hiding. The place is packed and so full of smoke that the fire alarms must have been disabled. We fight our way to the bar and order drinks from a server who is forced every few minutes to break off from her job and suck hard on an inhaler. Several unattended children run wild around the tables. Real Madrid scores goals on an overhead screen, as a jukebox blares Lady Gaga singing "Just Dance."

A menu offers Cervantes soup, Cervantes tapas, Cervantes spinach with chickpeas, or Cervantes dry-cured ham. We settle for a plate of Cervantes tapas and then hike back through the windswept streets to our suite of rooms, breathing in deeply and looking ahead to the day, now imminent, when Spain introduces a ban on smoking in its restaurants and bars. It takes us half an hour to unlock and then secure the iron gate and the wooden door. But it will take a lot longer for the pungent smell of stale smoke to work its way out of our hair and clothes.

{ELEVEN}

THE NEXT DAY IS SUNDAY, SO BREAKFAST IN THE MONASTERY—
normally served at 8:00 a.m.—is deláyed two and a half hours so
the nuns can complete the first few rounds of their morning prayers.
For us, that means we have time to kill. We could loll around in our
suite, but the radiator there, while gurgling like a contented baby, is
not throwing out much warmth, so we repair to the Panda and sit
with the engine running and the heater turned on full. A cold wind
blows, carrying what feels like the first hint of winter.

At 10:30, I slip the car into gear and drive the fifty yards
around the corner to the front of the monastery. The main doors
are sealed tight just as they were when we first arrived, but as I
pull to a stop one of them edges open a crack and I catch a fleet-
ing glimpse of a white-robed figure on the other side. I take this as
a signal that breakfast is about to be served, so we cross the street
and once more step into the gloom.

We stand dumbly facing the five French-farce doors until
the middle one opens and a different nun steps out—not Sister

María, but an even plumper version with a ripple of chins that cascade onto her habit in a waterfall of flesh. She points to one of the other doors and signals us to go through. A label beside it says the door will open to the *locutorio pequeño*, or small visitors' room. The nun glides silently backwards and disappears through the middle door, closing it softly behind her.

We step through our door and enter a boxlike room. The ceiling soars high above us—which is fortunate, since the room, already small, is divided in two by a row of black-iron bars. Numerous crosses hang on the walls along with the inevitable pictures of morbid saints, and a list of rules, pinned to the door, instructs us to "Make this place your home while you are here."

In our half of the cage, a round table—with a couple of chairs beside it—has been pushed up against the bars. It's a bistro-style table that would not be out of place on a Parisian boulevard, and right now it has been beautifully laid for breakfast for two, with a floral tablecloth that sweeps to the floor, two sets of white china plates, cups and saucers, elegant cutlery, a jug of water, a selection of tea bags, and a couple of cloth *servilletas* that are neatly embroidered with green-leafed flowers.

A door opens in the other half of the cage and our nun reappears, carrying a steaming kettle. She also sports wire-rimmed glasses that she wears at a cockeyed angle as if someone has hit her in the head with a left hook. With a gesture, she invites us to sit, then passes the kettle through a gap in the bars that has been created specifically to allow transactions like this. As we pour boiling water over our tea bags and hand the kettle back,

I can't help thinking that I've witnessed this scene before—in every prison movie I've ever watched. At this point, I should be handing the nun a homemade cake with a file or perhaps a revolver baked inside.

She disappears through her door and reemerges a few minutes later, this time carrying a tray. She threads a long loaf of French bread through the bars towards us, followed by a dish of margarine and a fresh pot of strawberry jam. Then she pulls up a chair in her part of the cage and settles in to watch us eat, like a keeper observing feeding time at the zoo.

Her name, she tells us, is Sister Victoria Morales, and she was born right here in El Toboso. She is seventy-five years old now, and entered the monastery when she was just twenty-one. "That was when I committed to God. On October 15, 1955." She is very precise about this date—giving the month and day, not just the year—since clearly it is the most important date in her life.

I had expected her to speak in a soft, modulated tone—if she was willing to speak at all—but she has a foghorn of a voice as if she's not used to speaking out loud and has not yet mastered the volume control. Or perhaps she talks mainly to other elderly nuns who are at least partially—or possibly totally—deaf.

She has three real-life sisters, she booms at us, who still live in the town. They come to see her occasionally, sitting where we are now and shouting small talk through the bars. For her part, Sister Victoria—although cloistered—is allowed to leave the monastery if she needs to visit a doctor or attend a family member's funeral. She frowns hard and clenches her jaw when I ask her what she

knows of the outside world. The eight nuns who live in the monastery do not subscribe to a newspaper, she says, nor do they read
any magazines. "But we do get some religious pamphlets, and we
also share a television set"—but only, it transpires, to watch religious programs or to catch up with the religious news.

"We sometimes play videos," she shouts. "But only religious
ones. And we do have a telephone. Also a computer"—which
allows the nuns to send and receive e-mails. "But we don't use it
much. We're far too busy. And anyway, if something important
happens in the world, we get to hear about it somehow."

That may be. But later, in response to our questions, it
becomes clear that she cannot name either the president of Spain
or the president of the United States.

☩

With breakfast over, I ask Sister Victoria if she is able to show
us any of the other parts of the monastery. She's ambivalent at
first, but then concedes that there are "one or two treasures" we
might be able to see in the monastery's *museo*. Like Sister María
the day before, she asks us to walk around the outside walls and
wait by the locked double doors of the monastery's church. We do
as we're told, and a few minutes later, she creaks open one of the
doors and lets us inside.

The church, as we might have expected, is cold, and exhibits
the clear signs of rising damp. Several splotches of mold pattern
its walls while worrying cracks mar the ceiling close to the base

162

of the dome. Behind the altar, there's an ornate *retablo*, but the rest of the church is plain—surprisingly so, given the Baroque era in which it was built. A few dark canvases hang on the walls, portraits, for the most part, of memorable Trinitarians, suffering saints, local dignitaries, and a small smattering of bishops and priests, but they're mainly notable for the large gaps that exist between them.

"We had many more paintings once," Sister Victoria says, "but they were all stolen during the war"—the Spanish Civil War, she means, when the church was used by the Republicans as a makeshift garrison. She leads us around the altar, then along the far side of the nave, moving slowly with a lumbering, shuffling gait. "There's no money for upkeep," she says. "Not anymore. We get nothing from the government. No real help at all."

We pass a carved statue of a black Jesus—a clone of the purple-robed figure in the chapel upstairs—then enter a small room that's opposite the main double doors. "We sometimes pray in here," Sister Victoria says, "because it's warmer. It's much too cold in the church, especially in winter."

She shows us a reliquary that supposedly contains the bones of Ángela María la Concepción, the nun who founded the monastery back in the seventeenth century. The reliquary is old and possibly of silver, but neither it—nor its contents—constitutes what I would normally think of as "treasures."

But then Sister Victoria leads us through a side door out of the church and farther into the heart of the monastery. We're not supposed to be here, so Sister Victoria makes us scurry along one side of the cloister. It's an oasis of light in the cloister, with a profusion of plants and flowers hiding the frescoes and over-flowing the handmade chests and benches that line the walls—a glimpse of the engaging ambience that surrounds the nuns as they go about their daily routine.

We follow her through an archway in a stone wall that must be three or four feet thick to the veritable trove of "treasures" the monastery has collected over the centuries, now on display in its *museo*. And finally I understand why Sister María was so insistent that we lock all our doors.

As might be expected, there are many renditions of Jesus on show. One is a powerful wooden head that was carved in the sev-enteenth century. Another is a full-body statue—also in wood—that shows Jesus nailed to his cross; it dates from the early part of the sixteenth century. And hanging nearby is an exquisite por-trait of Jesus with his crown of thorns, looking pale, drawn, and splattered with blood.

The portrait is titled *Ecce Homo,* or *Behold the Man*—the phrase Pontius Pilate reportedly used when he paraded Jesus in front of the mob that was baying for his death.

"It's Flemish," Sister Victoria says, "and very valuable."

I lean closer and read the plaque beside it. It's a small portrait, sixteen inches by eleven inches. *Oleo sobre tabla*—oil on wood. Painted in the first half of the sixteenth century. By Aelbrecht Bouts. A Flemish painter I know little about. But when I later google his name I find that his works hang in a large number of prestigious galleries across Europe and the United States, including the National Gallery of Denmark, the Fitzwilliam Museum in Cambridge, England, the Metropolitan Museum of Art in New York, and the Los Angeles County Museum of Art. I also discover that his works sell for hundreds of thousands of dollars, yet this one here is viewed, almost exclusively, by eight elderly and impoverished nuns.

"It was stolen during the war," Sister Victoria says—again referring to the Spanish Civil War—"but was later found in Madrid. We managed to get it back," she says.

It's a compelling painting. The artist has made Jesus appear so vulnerable that even the most heartless non-believer can relate to his pain. Christ's eyes are heavy with suffering and show his fatigue, but his face shines like a light against the dark palette that Bouts has chosen for the background.

The *Ecce Homo* overlooks a room that's full of glass-topped display cases, the nearest of which is stuffed with chalices, pyxides, censers, and other sacred vessels fashioned out of silver or gold. Sister Victoria points to one in particular. "It was given to the monastery by Philip V in 1725. For Christmas," she says.

A table beside it has a display of ancient religious texts. One at the front catches my eye. It's a hymnal, open to show a double-page spread. The pages are wrinkled and yellowed around the edges, but the illustrations—and the capital letters, backed by gold, which begin each line—are beautifully rendered and manage to retain the full force of their original color.

"There's another one over there," Sister Victoria tells me. I look across to the other side of the table and see a matching tome that's bound in leather with metal trim protecting the corners. "Both in Latin," she says, "and both sixteenth century."

Other books on the table are open to show their title pages. I make a note of some of their dates: MDCLXXVI, or 1676; MDCCLXXII, or 1772; and MDCCLXXXIX, which I think is 1789.

She leads us into an adjoining room, past a wooden harp that was originally owned by the monastery's founder. "It's seventeenth century," she says in passing, then points to a carved piece of wood that hangs near the doorway. "That's eleventh century. Part of the altar from a church that used to be on this site."

She waves her arms in the air and invites us to look around—at the tapestries on the walls, the seventeenth-century portrait of Santa Teresa, and at the display cases of gold-embroidered tunics, capes, and other vestments that bishops and priests used to wear when they said Mass. "They're eighteenth century," she tells us. So almost new.

One of the vestments she points to is expertly finished with a decorative trim of gold. It was a gift to the monastery from Luisa de Parma, the wife of Charles IV—"in 1789," Sister Victoria says, then frowns slightly before adding, "A difficult time for Europe," as if the French Revolution and Napoleon's invasion of Spain were part of her personal history rather than events she has read about in a book.

She looks sadly around the room like someone surveying the wreck of a burgled home. "So much was stolen," she says. "The army came and turned our monastery into a barracks. We lost so much. We've managed to get a lot of it back. But there's still so much that's missing, so much that we'll never see again."

I nod my head in sympathy. I'm sure what she says is true. But the "little" that remains is enough for me. I feel privileged just to be here.

✠

Later that night, I return to the small chapel with the purple-robed figure of Jesus and look through the grilles into the church below. It's easy to imagine one of the nuns sitting up here for long periods in silent contemplation. I'm not sure I'd want to do that, but a few years ago I read a biography of the British scientist Humphrey Davy, who is best remembered today for the eponymous lamp he invented for miners. For most of his life, Davy was a hardened rationalist, a passionate proponent of the scientific method for determining knowledge, but near the end of his days, he wrote a letter to his wife in which he said, "The art of living happy is, I believe, the art of being agreeably deluded."

He also said that "faith in all things is superior to reason, which after all, is but a dead weight in advanced life, though as the pendulum to the clock in youth."

I think Davy was right. At the time—this was in 1828—he was living in Austria and spending his days "writing, fishing and taking morphine," the drug of choice for many of the nineteenth century's greatest thinkers, so he might just have been high. But either way, Davy's sentiment made me think that I, too, have reached a point in my life where I'd like to surrender the power of reason in exchange for the agreeable delusion of faith.

This morning over breakfast in the *locutorio pequeño*, I asked Sister Victoria what keeps her soldiering on after more than fifty-five years of the same daily routine, endlessly performing the roster of prayers, the Liturgy of the Hours, that all nuns (and monks, too) must complete if they're to comply with canon law of the Catholic Church. It's a difficult life, made deliberately harder by the fact that the nuns have agreed not to talk to one another except during meals. So where does her faith come from, I wanted to know, and how does she manage to sustain it?

When I put these questions to her, she reached through the bars of her cage and clutched my arm in a vice-like grip. "Prayer is important to me," she said. "God hears me when I pray. I know he does. He gave me life. So I know he must hear me." Her face was radiant, her expression intense. "This is the best life for me. I could not possibly live any other."

Yes, but where does her faith come from? I persisted. And how can I hope to acquire it?

But she was not about to give me direction. All she was willing to say was, "Faith comes from God. Where else can it come from? It can come only from God."

This is the same answer we were given by Sister María Federica, the nun we met in Vallbona de les Monges, and to me it makes little sense, because to get your faith from God, you must first believe in God, which means, of course, that you already have the faith that you want him to give you.

Not for the first time on this journey, I feel as if I'm talking to people who have found the answers to every serious question I've asked myself, yet for some unknown reason they are unwilling—or unable—to share those answers with me.

El Monasterio de la Santa María
de las Escalonias

✠

*Cistercians of the Strict Observance,
aka Trappist*

{TWELVE}

From El Toboso, we head south along the A4 to enter Andalucía—in my view the most fascinating region of Spain because of its unique, mix-and-match mongrel past. It's part Tartessian, Phoenician, Greek, Carthaginian, Roman, Vandal, Visigoth, Christian, Jewish, and Muslim, and you don't have to look very far to see traces of nearly every one of its disparate roots.

In Córdoba—once the capital of the Muslim Caliphate and so once the most learned city in Europe (at one time, the Emir's library held as many as 400,000 books, more, probably, than the sum total in the rest of the continent)—we stop briefly to visit the birthplaces of Averroes (a Muslim) and Maimonides (a Jew), who, along with Aquinas (a Christian), tried to reconcile knowledge and faith. That was back in the twelfth and thirteenth centuries, when Europe was mired in ignorance and superstition. Knowledge was almost nonexistent, so it was still possible to align it with faith without undue twisting or distortion. The basic thinking then was that scripture is truth—so it has nothing to fear from knowledge, even if that knowledge is gained through reason.

Knowledge, of course, keeps on increasing, while for some, faith remains fixed, locked into the past. Today, knowledge has increased to such an extent that reconciliation with faith is all but impossible, although that hasn't stopped some people from trying. In the seventeenth century, Archbishop James Ussher famously declared that the Earth was created by God on Saturday, October 22, in 4004 B.C. at about six o'clock in the evening (Greenwich Mean Time, presumably). A century or so later, it was clear to many that this calculation was slightly off target—especially when buried fossils were found that were evidently hundreds of thousands of years older than Ussher claimed the Earth to be. Knowledge was at odds with faith. But rather than adjust their beliefs to meet this newfound knowledge, Ussher's followers adjusted their knowledge—maintaining that the ancient fossils had been placed in the Earth by God, as part of a test of Mankind's faith. The buried fossils did not, therefore, bring into question the age of the Earth. Instead they served to further confirm the existence of God.

As Mark Twain once said, "Faith is believing what you know ain't so."

☩

We also take time in Córdoba to visit the Mezquita-Catedral, one of the most memorable buildings in the world. Originally a mosque, its roof is supported by a seemingly endless forest of marble pillars topped by double tiers of red-and-white, candy-striped, horseshoe arches. Venture far enough into this forest and you eventually arrive at an exquisitely crafted mihrab, decorated with mosaics and delicate filigree plasterwork. But the real surprise of this exemplary Muslim edifice is that right in its heart—and soaring above it—stands a full-size Catholic cathedral, plunked down like an alien space ship soon after Christians retook the city in 1236 during the Reconquista.

The cathedral was intended as a swaggering attempt to show that "My religion is better than yours," but a contemporary slant on the way it has been blended into the mosque might now more empathetically say, "We might be different in fundamental ways, but here at least we have learned to share."

We push on a few more miles, following the course of the Guadalquivir River to the small town of Posadas, which is close to our next destination—the Cistercian Monasterio de la Santa María de las Escalonias. On the drive south, I've been mulling over my dissatisfaction with the answers I've been getting to my questions about faith—where does it come from, and how can it be found? Like a dog chasing its own tail, these answers have turned in meaningless circles. I know that Jesus, in Luke 17:20-21, said, "The Kingdom of God is within you," but to say that "faith in God can come only from God" is to presuppose the answer before any question has even been posed. Perhaps, I think, the problem lies not with the answers but with the fact that they've come from elderly nuns who live cloistered lives, surrounded by people who think like they do and so endorse—rather than challenge—their views.

The community we're about to visit at Las Escalonias is likely to be different, since it follows a branch of the Cistercian Order that goes out of its way to practice "strict observance." To my mind, that means I can expect the residents there to be even more serious and committed than the monks and nuns we've so far encountered, with no fudging or sidestepping of the difficult issues.

If there is any kind of pattern in the development of monastic life in Europe, it is this: Someone founds an Order that has strict rules governing how God should be honored. Over time the strict rules are allowed to bend until someone else breaks away to found a new Order that reaffirms the severity of the original rules. Thus in the sixth century, monasticism in Europe was first given its shape and character by Benedict of Nursia, who became disgusted with the dissolute way of life that prevailed in Rome when he was studying in that city. He abandoned his work and left town to become a hermit, living in a cave in nearby Subiaco, where he was soon joined by other like-minded people. A few years later Benedict moved to Monte Cassino near Naples to found the monastery that is still the motherhouse of the now-worldwide Benedictine Order, and while there he finalized his celebrated rules on which all Western monasticism is based.

These rules—collated by Benedict, but probably derived from the work of others—are collectively known as the "Rule of St. Benedict," "the Rule," or just the initials "RB." They are relatively few in number (when put together they make up a slim volume of about eighty pages), and they are not meant to be severe or unduly restricting (Benedict, in his Prologue, said they constitute "a little Rule for beginners" and contain "nothing harsh or burdensome"). They do, however, constitute a guide that, for thousands of Christians over hundreds of years, has helped shape the way that life should be led.

I must confess that I sometimes feel a secret need for a set of rules like this. They give purpose and direction to what otherwise might seem like a meaningless and random walk through life. Without a religion—and the rules that go with it—you have to compile guidelines of your own. That's possible, of course; but it requires a lot of thought, and it carries with it the risk that your rules might be bent or abandoned (since you are both player and referee) if they become too hard to follow.

Benedict's rules primarily cover the way prayer, meditative reading, and manual work should form the backbone of monastic life. They also demand that monks (and nuns, too) live a communal life, learning to accept other people for what they are, no matter how maddening their personal quirks. They require that monks should spend their entire lives within the same community (the one in which they took their vows), and they demand that monks obey a spiritual leader, an elected abbot who is viewed not just as a father figure but also as a representative of Christ on Earth. They also determine how monks should eat, dress, sleep, pray, and recruit new members, and they state that monks should give hospitality to any passing or in-need strangers ("let everyone who comes be received as Christ").

Over the centuries, standards slipped and the rules were eased, as the Benedictine monks grew rich, fat, and comfortable, often hiring other people to do their work for them, and in some cases to say their prayers and other devotions, too. So in the tenth century, a separate Benedictine Order was launched—at Cluny in France—as an offshoot of the first. It was different from the original Order in that its authority was centralized—not vested in each individual community. This centralized structure gave the Abbot of Cluny significant power, and with the power inevitably came the attendant corruption. So new Orders—like the Carthusians and, more significantly, the Cistercians—were soon founded in an attempt to get back to basics and reaffirm the Rule.

The Cistercians proved to be especially successful. They wore white in contrast to the black habits worn by the Benedictines and Cluniacs (and so became known as the "white," rather than "black," monks). They had one lead house at Cîteaux, near Dijon in France, founded in 1098 by St. Robert of Molesme. But each of their monasteries was a self-governing community. Other Orders also sprang up at about the same time—including those of the Carmelites, Dominicans, and Franciscans—but these new Orders were fundamentally different again, because their members were friars, not monks. That meant they were not cloistered, but instead went out into the world to do good works and to spread the word of the Gospels.

As the Cistercian influence extended across Europe, standards again began to fall, so another Order was spun off—one that was far more rigorous and strict. It was founded by Armand de Rancé at La

Trappe Abbey in Normandy, France, and in 1892, with the approval of the Pope, it split completely from the original Cistercians and became an autonomous branch. In 1902, it took on the formal name of the Order of the Cistercians of the Strict Observance, but to most people it is best known by the name that's derived from the abbey where the Order was spawned—the Trappists.

In my view, Trappists are likely to be hard core—more committed to honoring God, and more understanding of their own faith. Already, the ones we expect to encounter at El Monasterio de la Santa María de las Escalonias have given a hint of their greater devotion in the correspondence we exchanged with them, when we were trying to book a room. In response to our initial inquiry, we received an e-mail from *Hermano*, or Brother, Abdón saying "our monastic *hospedería* is a place of retreat and prayer" (meaning: this is not a hotel); "we are situated in the country not in a town" (so if you're planning to party, go elsewhere); "we shut our gates at 9:30 in the evening" (nightlife is off the cards); and "our guests like to rest and have a peaceful time before they go to bed" (so bring a book to read, or better yet, two). As a considerate afterthought, Brother Abdón also informed us that "five o'clock is a good time to arrive because Vespers starts at 6:30 and that will give you time to settle into your room before making your way to the church."

So far on this journey, we have been only dabbling in the shallows of monastic life. At Las Escalonias that will no longer be possible. Brother Abdón has made it clear that we will be expected to participate fully in the devotional life of the community and not just be granted our normal observer status. It's time, I now think, to plunge into the deep end and see if we will sink or swim.

✛

Outside the town of Posadas, we turn off the highway and head along a dirt road towards the monastery. As I wrestle the Panda around a series of potholes, I realize I'm expecting a setting as austere and forbidding as *Wuthering Heights*, but as the dirt of the road gives way to dust—a sign that we are nearing the monastery—all I can see is grove after grove of flourishing trees. Orange trees, with early-ripened fruit scattered around them like spangled fire opals. We are only five miles from the A431 road— and just twenty-two miles from Córdoba—but already we are deep into fertile country.

I stop by an iron gate that is slung between two white-and-yellow-painted walls with the name of Las Escalonias spelled out on them in blue-and-white ceramic tile. To the left of the gate there's a small whitewashed shrine with a red-tiled roof and purple flowers creeping up its walls. It's dedicated to St. Isidro, the Spanish patron saint of farmers. The gate is open so we drive on and soon catch a glimpse of more substantial buildings ahead. We're on a long driveway now, lined on both sides by hundred-foot-high eucalyptus trees, their bark peeling like a bad sunburn, branches meeting high overhead to form a natural Gothic arch. Sunlight comes dappling through the leaves, so the effect is less *Wuthering Heights* and more like Tara in *Gone with the Wind*.

At the end of the driveway, we turn a corner and see the monastery for the first time. It's a colonial-style building, freshly painted in white with an ochre-yellow trim around the windows and doors. We sweep through a gravel forecourt and see a sign for the *hospedería* that points us around to the back, past a profusion of tropical plants and the giant-handed leaves of mature fig trees. Like the main building of the monastery, the *hospedería* is in excellent repair—a two-story, whitewashed structure with neat brick trim highlighting its many windows and doors. I pull into a parking space behind it, next to three other cars that are already there, and we go inside.

After the bright sunlight it takes a moment for our eyes to adjust, but when they do we see we are standing in a welcoming lobby that could be the entrance hall of an English country house. Several armchairs, a deep-cushioned leather sofa, and an oak side-table have been arranged companionably around a wood-burning stove. There are planters and pots of fresh-cut flowers, as well as a bowl of walnuts set on a larger table near the door. Hung on one of the white-plaster walls is a reproduction of van Gogh's *Sunflowers*, which is flanked—on two of the other walls—by shelves of magazines and books. The fourth wall has been given over to a reception desk with guest book and bell. There is no receptionist, but there are three other people, all men, who, it would seem, are fellow guests.

At first sight, they look an odd trio, and it appears we may have caught them in the act of committing a crime, as they are frozen into place in startled poses. One of the men, short, with broken teeth, is armed with a pair of garden shears that he's tucked under one elbow. The second man looks to be a recovering alcoholic, with a road map of veins covering his mottled skin, while the third—a tall, thin, pallid man who holds himself as stiff and erect as a mannequin—can only be a serial killer. He lurks in the shadows of a corner, then slides towards us like an apparition. He's dressed entirely in black, and wears a toupee—the worst I think I've ever seen—that's squashed on his head like a roadkill squirrel. It is a rich red-brown, as thick and wiry as a nylon doormat, and makes no attempt to blend in with the strands of gray of his natural hair.

The short man with the shears nods a silent hello, as does the recovering alcoholic. The serial killer, however, just holds his peace.

I look around at the rest of the room. Tucked into a corner there's a vending machine that dispenses six kinds of coffee, and beside that stands another machine that I think yields soft drinks—Coca-Cola, Fanta, and Agua con Gas—but on closer examination also promises to bestow sinfully large cans of ice-cold beer. On the walls by the reception there are several signs mandating *silencio*, as well as a short list of rules that we're asked to follow. One says, *El silencio durante el día*; another reminds us that, *La hospedería monástica no es un hotel*; while a third says, *Procure ser punctual en las horas de las comidas y al recogerse en su habitación*, which roughly translates as, Try to be punctual for meals and go to bed at the proper time.

I'm about to ask the man with the shears if there are any Trappist monks around (the recovering alcoholic has stepped outside for a smoke) when two of them appear in the doorway. The older of the two—he looks about fifty, but we later find he's fifty-seven—is heavy-set with closely cropped hair and the inevitable pair of wire-rimmed glasses. He introduces himself as Padre José, but quickly tells us to call him "Pepe." His sidekick—considerably younger and also trimmer—is called Vicente. "He's still a postulant," Pepe says.

Neither of the two men is dressed in the white habit and black scapular I had expected. Instead, they both wear civvies—in Pepe's case a pair of prison blue pants, matching blue sweater, and sneakers, while Vicente sports what looks like a sweatshirt hoodie, but is really a postulant's jacket, which he has paired with loudly checked pants that could be the bottom half of a set of pajamas.

Pepe does the talking for them both, telling us he's originally from Granada where he worked as a parish priest, but when he decided he wanted "to get closer to God," he applied to come here to Las Escalonias. "That was about ten years ago." He still studies theology, but otherwise his life is entirely devoted to work, piety, and prayer. He's relaxed and friendly when he tells us this, but he also has a wary tone as if he suspects we might be using his monastery for reasons other than worship—perhaps as a hotel. The monastery does get a steady stream of visitors, he says, and can accommodate up to about thirty at any one time. Some of the people who come are fellow monks from other communities; others are laypeople hoping to better connect with God; and the rest are non-believers who are searching for—well, for something else, he says, and looks at us carefully.

"You mean they're people like us," I say, and we all laugh because now the elephant in the room has been acknowledged.

He leads us upstairs past several more van Gogh–style paintings. On the second floor, we pause for a moment by another arrangement of sofas and chairs beneath a large canvas of monks diligently working. It's an original painting, Pepe says, and the monks depicted are the ones who founded Las Escalonias in 1986, setting it up as a sister house to the Cistercian Monasterio Santa María la Real de la Oliva—better known simply as La Oliva— in the northern region of Navarre. The monks in the painting are shown with the tools of their trade—prayer books, hymnals, scythes, an organ—in a kind of reverse symbolism that illustrates the attributes of their lives rather than the manner of their deaths.

Pepe takes us along a corridor and stops outside Room 15. We push open the door and go in. It's a cozy room with a glowing, red-tile floor and twin beds, covered in red, green, and beige bedspreads, which are separated by a table with a brass reading lamp standing on top. Above that hangs a Byzantine-style print of the Madonna and Child, while above the door there's a smart new heater controlled by a remote. There's plenty of light streaming in from the window that overlooks the orange groves, and there are two desks and chairs where we can sit, contemplate, doodle, or even write. The en suite bathroom is equally bright, as well as spotlessly clean and well-appointed—right down to the large fluffy towels. Even a Helmsley or Trump would have no cause for complaint. We could easily be in a secular retreat, a well-run bed-and-breakfast or—dare I say it—a modern hotel.

‡

Pepe has confirmed that Vespers starts at 6:30 p.m. and clearly the expectation is that we will attend. So with dusk beginning to gather, we track the white wall of the monastery that leads from the *hospedería* to the main monastery building and, no doubt, to the church. We follow a gravel path flanked by hedges past small courtyards filled with flowers, stone statuettes, and large wooden tubs planted with exotic palms. We're nervously early, which is just as well, as we inadvertently overshoot the church and arrive instead at the monastery store.

Two women are hard at work behind the counter, stuffing unshelled *nogales*, or walnuts, into nylon-mesh bags. I say "hello" but they both look uncomprehending. A robed monk shrouded in his cowl appears through a side door. He cuts a mean figure, evoking Salem witch hunts, the Inquisition, and Mexico's Day of the Dead.

"They can't understand," he says, nodding at the women. "They're Romanian, and don't speak Spanish."

A third woman who's stacking the filled nylon-mesh bags offers me a walnut, holding it on the palm of her hand the way she might hold out an apple towards a horse. "Here," she says. "Try one. They're good for the brain." She puts the walnut on the counter and whacks it with a stone as if killing a cockroach. The shell splits wide open, spilling its contents onto the floor.

"At this time of year," she says, "we have hundreds of walnuts. Hundreds of thousands of walnuts that we pack into bags and sell by the kilo."

She shows us some of the other products the monastery offers for sale: pots of marmalade made from the trillions of oranges we've seen in the groves all around and jars of honey produced by bees that feed exclusively on the orange-tree blossoms. She holds my attention until I'm distracted by the racks of wine the store also sells, which I can see over her shoulder.

"We've a *vino reserva*," the woman tells me, "that's produced by La Oliva, our parent monastery in Navarre. We sell it for seven euros a bottle, and serve it here in the monastery with meals. The other wine," she says, "comes from the Monasterio de San Pedro de Cardeña, another Trappist monastery near Burgos. That sells for eight euros a bottle."

I look along the shelves at the other items that are offered for sale: huge slabs of chocolate, large rounds of cheese, the obligatory key rings with Jesus attached, some painted jugs decorated with angels, a selection of books—*Seven Days of Prayer, Sing Jesus a New Song, Truths of the Catholic Church, Contemplative Community*—postcards featuring popular saints, and much-in-demand cigarette lighters imprinted with colorful images of the Virgin.

"There's no drive-by traffic," the woman says, stating the obvious. "So we rely on word of mouth and the fact that all of the items we sell are in demand."

I nod in agreement. The key rings, I know, are popular with Spanish drivers. They allow them to hurtle along at breakneck speed, secure in the knowledge that a dangling Jesus shoved into the ignition will save and protect them from accident and harm.

The clang of bells—a sign that Vespers will start in fifteen minutes—rules out further conversation, so we head back to where we've been told we will find the church. I realize now why we missed it before, because it's not like a church at all, but appears to be a converted barn that a yuppie has renovated as a weekend retreat. It has modest doors off a small courtyard; its roof is low and terra-cotta-tiled; and its windows are plain glass fitted into pleasing rounded arches.

We find the recovering alcoholic grabbing a last-minute drag on a cigarette before he enters the smoke-free zone of the church, and follow him in. The woman from the store has tagged along, rightly assessing we're in need of guidance. The monastery, she tells us, was once a *finca*—a country house or estate—that the owners found they could no longer afford to maintain. To crawl out from under their debt, they donated the buildings and grounds to the Trappist monks in La Oliva. A few of them—the ones depicted in the *hospedería* painting—moved into the property and over a period of about twelve years, finishing in the year 2000, converted it into a magnificent monastery complete with cloister, refectory, cells, and a laundry, which the monks now operate on a commercial basis.

"The church was one of the buildings they transformed," the woman tells us. "It was once a *vacaría*"—literally a cowshed.

She leads us into the darkest corner of the church, where stacks of books covering the various Offices are stored. Apparently we're meant to take a copy of the book that's appropriate to the service we're attending, so this being Vespers we need to take a copy of the *Oficio de Vísperas*. We're up to speed on that, but we're also supposed to note down the numbers of the psalms that will be sung during the service. They have been scrawled in red marker-pen on a whiteboard pinned to the wall above the books and, following the store lady's instructions, we write them down on one of the scraps of paper that a monk has thoughtfully placed by the books. There are only four, I'm relieved to see: 112, 34, 48, and all the sevens, 77.

We take a pew, with the store lady sitting a few rows behind. The altar in front of us is a simple stone block on a raised platform of shiny dark tile. There is no fancy *retablo* behind it—just an elegant statue, cleverly backlit, of Mary holding the baby Jesus, positioned on top of a short stone plinth. The pews, which run the length of the church, have been made from a rich dark wood that blends into the tiles on the floor. The altar candelabra are bronze, not gold. The silver ciborium, housed in a recess, adds a touch of glitz, but everything else is elegant, tasteful, and under-stated in a spare, Bauhaus way.

The wall behind Mary has, I notice, been painted an ochre-yellow that matches the trim around the windows and doors of the main monastery building. This color is probably not a random selection, but is instead a deliberate choice, since tradition has it that the Devil abhors yellow and will not come into a build-ing that's painted that color. How this was established I'm not quite sure, but it seems to me to represent a point where religion morphs into superstition.

The other fellow guests from the *hospedería* have followed us into the church and taken their seats near the back. The short man has lost his shears, but the serial killer still wears his toupee.

The monks file in using a door that leads from the cloister, and as they bow toward the altar I realize I could be at risk of seeing them as a type—elderly, balding, a little overweight, and bespectacled with wire-frame glasses. These monks, however, have a few younger ones sprinkled in their midst. I count ten of them altogether—just enough to fill the front row of pews. They're all dressed in long white habits—except for Vincente, the Postulant, who is still in his hoodie and loud checked pants.

There is a long moment of silence while we individually think our various thoughts. Mine are brought to a halt by the two-tone chime of a bell—like a cuckoo clock—which marks the start of the service.

Immediately the monks all begin to chant. I open my *Oficio de Vísperas* at the appropriate page but can find no sign of the psalm I'm meant to be singing, so I just follow along, lip-synching any words that come to mind, but not unfortunately the ones that the monks are chanting: "My shield is God who saves those of good heart . . ." "Jesus is the judge of the villages . . ." "Judge me according to my fairness . . ." "Stop the wickedness of the Guilty and support the Innocent . . ." "God is a just judge . . ."

The monks remain seated while they chant—except when they come to a mention of "the Father, Son, and Holy Spirit," at which point they all rise to their feet and bow to the altar like the cast at the end of a Broadway play; then once again resume their places on their pew. For the most part, they have good voices, which they need since their chanting is unaccompanied. There is a small organ—played by one of the monks—but it sounds just a single note at the start of each psalm in order to set the key.

One of the monks gives a reading. Prayers are spoken and more psalms are chanted—and then the service is over. Several monks stay behind for further prayer, but we take our leave. The church is pleasantly warm and dry, but we're on the treadmill now so we need to hurry if we want to squeeze in *cena*, or supper, before it's time to show up for the next service.

✣

At 7:45 precisely, another bell rings out like a gong. Time for *cena*, so like Pavlov's dogs we file into the dining room off the lobby of the *hospedería*. Our three fellow guests are already there, along with Pepe and another monk who act as genial hosts. Stupidly, I show my secular colors by forgetting about grace, sitting down before thanking our Lord for what we are about to receive. Pepe clears his throat and I get back on my feet. I look around for the promised bottle of *vino reserva*, but no such luck. It's a glass or two of well water—or nothing.

As I might have expected when I pack my imagination away, our three companions prove to be disappointingly normal—and also excellent company for the next several days. The small man (no longer with shears) is Ricardo; he lives for six months of every year here in the monastery, working in the laundry and doing odd jobs around the property to help pay for his keep. Then he moves to a Clarissa monastery in Salamanca for the other six months of the year. It's his way of living the life of a monk without actually having to be one.

The recovering alcoholic really is a recovering alcoholic. He works as a cook in an addiction center in nearby Córdoba and comes here whenever he can because he credits God with helping him to bring his addiction under control. As for the serial killer—a gentle man we now know as Francisco—he is a respectable businessman who runs a *perfumería* in Aracena, not far from the Portuguese border. His frequent silences are as innocent as he is—the result of a hearing defect that sidelines him from most of the conversation.

Supper is eaten in something of a rush. It's a full meal of soup, celery in a sauce, miniature tuna *empanadas*, a tomato salad with bread, and for dessert yogurt and as many walnuts and oranges as you can eat, crack, peel, or stomach. There is just time to help with the cleanup before we all head back to the church for Compline at 8:45.

✠

It's pitch-black outside, but the monastery has an elaborate system of outdoor lighting that is fortunately simple to operate. With the press of a button on the *hospedería* wall the route to the church lights up like the path to Heaven. We set out at a brisk pace—it's only about two or three hundred yards—but I notice that Pepe and the other monk with whom we had dinner pile into a car and drive there. En route, we pass the recovering alcoholic, once again sucking on a last-minute cigarette.

We pick up a copy of the *Oficio de Compline* and jot down the designated numbers of the psalms, then settle into what we've already come to regard as "our" pew. As before, it's pleasantly warm in the church—even somnolently cozy. Our dinner companions join us, the monks file in, make the sign of the cross, bow towards the altar, and take their places in the front row. They've changed out of their habits and are now dressed in black and white cloaks with hoods (except for Vincente, who is still in his civvies). At 8:45 precisely, the cuckoo clock chimes, the organist strikes his single chord, and the service begins.

To my untrained ears, Compline sounds exactly like Vespers. We still can't crack the psalm-book code, but perhaps we don't have the right information. The monks stay seated except when taking their bows. The main difference between the services comes at the end, when we take our places in a conga line and snake towards the altar, bending low when we get there so one of the monks can sprinkle a shower of holy water onto the tops of our heads.

Compline lasts for half an hour, so we're back at the *hospedería* by about 9:30. Up in our room I set the alarm for 4:10 a.m. which is when we'll need to get up if we want to make it in time to Vigilia, the first service of the next day. We've told Pepe that we'll be there, since we're determined to walk the walk of a monk and not just talk the talk. For some reason that I can't quite fathom, I find myself looking forward to the experience.

{THIRTEEN}

When the alarm goes off, I'm deep into a dream and in no fit state to face a fellow human being, let alone God. But Vigilia calls and cannot be ignored. We dress quickly in *silencio*, throwing on our old clothes, then step out into the cold. I pull my fleece more tightly around me. There's a quarter-moon grinning above the orange groves, and a myriad of stars twinkling like diamonds in an inky-black sky. In fact, everywhere I look I see a deep cloudless space. So if God is up there, I have to admit he's done a bang-up job with his real estate. But down here on Earth, I do wish he would find a way to turn up the heat.

We press the button that lights the way to the church and set off, quietly grumbling. As the new kids on the block, we are overly eager, which means that once again we are early. We pick up the appropriate *Oficio* and settle into our familiar pew. A few people glide around—some of them monks. Some of them nod in our direction and I find myself experiencing an unexpected affinity with the brothers.

The rest of the monks file in from the cloister, many also look-ing as if they've dressed in a hurry, but all ten are present and cor-rect. The double chime of the cuckoo clock brings me out of the gentle state of half-sleep, half-wakefulness that I've fallen into, and the chanting starts. By sheer luck, my psalm book has opened at the right page so I can at least mumble along with the monks. "Judge me according to the innocence that is within me . . ." "You who sound the heart . . ." "You who are the just God . . ." "You who are the truth and light . . ." "The Father, Son, and Holy Spirit . . ."

The words and the chanting are soothing. Hypnotic. Like a relaxing drug or a Buddhist mantra. There's little in the way of meaning—at least to me—but the words and the phrases are repeated again and again, taking the mind away from itself so there's no requirement to think or even to be mentally present. I look up at the figure of Mary. The lights in the church have been turned down, but Mary is backlit and has a tall candle burning on either side of her. She looks serene and compassionate, in tune with herself and with the world around her.

The service lasts about forty-five minutes, so it's nearly 5:30 when we grope our way back to our room. There's not enough time to climb into bed for even a few minutes of sleep before we have to get back to the church for Laudes and Eucaristia. So we just shower and dress again—this time in clothes that match—and sit on our beds to stare at the floor. I nibble at a piece of chocolate that I've secreted away as comfort food, then, still in the dark, we return to the church and settle into our usual pew (still warm from Vigilia) and wait for the double chime and the monks to appear.

This time they file in from the sacristy, rather than the cloister. The lead monk, dressed entirely in red, is followed by four other monks in long white habits with blood-red sashes; and they, in turn, are followed by four more monks clothed entirely in white with their cowls up shrouding their faces. At the rear is Vincente, making do with his civvies and his pale-gray hoodie.

The lead monk seats himself behind the altar and the service begins. This is the big one of the day, Laudes and Eucaristia combined, complete with wine and wafers. The monks must have performed this service many thousands of times before, but they perform it again with all the freshness of an opening night. Each one has his part to play. And not once does anyone make eye contact—with another monk or with us—as that would break the spell and lead to the wrong kind of communication; person to person, instead of monk to God.

There is more chanting and bowing towards the altar. I struggle to keep awake, but notice, with some satisfaction, that Pepe is yawning and the head of one of the other monks has fallen so far forward onto his chest that, from behind, he appears to have been topped. An hour later the service draws to a close, and I glance up at the windows to see the first streaks of dawn cutting through the gloom.

There is time to step outside—but not to return to our room—as we only have fifteen minutes before the next service, Tercia, is due to get under way. We loiter in the courtyard like customers waiting for a bar to open. No one seems inclined to talk so we scuff our feet, retie our shoe laces, and examine the many plants until the warning bell rings and we step back into the church and retake our pews.

The monks reappear—in a new set of robes—and we're off again. Tercia lasts a scant ten minutes—which to my emerging standards is not long enough to get properly warmed up. As the last of the chanting fades away, we trudge back to the *hospedería* for breakfast, which is served as a buffet. Cereal, toast, marmalade, coffee, walnuts, oranges, walnuts again, and still more oranges. Ricardo, however, appears to have a special dietary requirement. He consumes a dozen cloves of raw garlic doused in olive oil, which he mops up with thick doorsteps of bread.

"Healthy," he says between mouthfuls. "Good for the heart. For the *corazón*."

I nod in agreement. I'm quite sure, I tell him, that if he keeps this up, his heart will outlive him by at least twenty years.

✛

With breakfast cleared away, we have a short break, and since it's a bright sunny day, we head outside and set off in the opposite direction from the church to wander along the grassy lanes that thread their way through the acres and acres of orange groves. As we double back to the far side of the main monastery building, we bump into one of the monks—a portly man about fifty years old who has dispensed with his habit and is now dressed in a pair of blue overalls and red slippers that have two holes on the top where his big toes have poked through. He introduces himself as

Brother Eugenio and tells us he's working a shift in the monastery's laundry.

"We take in a lot of laundry," he says. "From local businesses like hotels, as well as from the Red Cross hospital in Palma del Río," which is not far from here.

The laundry, apparently, is the monastery's main source of income, along with the *hospedería*, the gift shop, and the sales of oranges and walnuts.

I ask him if he always wanted to be a monk, and he shakes his head quickly.

"No, no," he says. "I used to live in Madrid, right in the center. I earned a lot of money then, working for Otis Elevator. And I never had to work too hard. It was a good life, and an easy life."

I make the mistake of embarking on a joke about elevators going up and down and perhaps lifting him closer to God, but my Spanish isn't up to it and I realize it's not even funny. So I search for a new topic and ask him about the orange groves all around us.

He again shakes his head. "The oranges here are of poor quality," he tells us, "so they're very hard to sell. The people here only want to eat oranges that come from Valencia"—the province on Spain's Mediterranean coast, which lies opposite the party island of Ibiza and is well known for its fruit.

We wander on towards the main gate, past fields planted with endless rows of walnut trees. Another monk sits on a bench by the driveway with his nose buried in a well-thumbed Bible. He still wears his habit from Tercia, but he has complemented it now with a straw boater that inexplicably has "Wild West Show" stenciled on the hatband in English. We keep going and once again enter the groves, where the trees are laden with oranges as big as grape-fruits. We walk down one row, and then along another, until we stumble onto a group of workers—Romanians, I suspect—who have been brought in to help with the harvest. One of them is hefting crates onto the flatbed of a truck, stacking them six high and grunting with the effort.

"Oranges," I say, as I sweep my hand at the trees all around us. He nods brusquely and grunts again, annoyed perhaps by this inane and obvious remark. "They're not very good?" I add, feeding him the sum total of what I know about the monastery's output.

He stops what he's doing and straightens up, crate in hand. "Not good?" he says indignantly. "Of course they're good. Some of the best in Spain." They're so good, he tells me, that they're in demand throughout the country—especially, he says, in the region of Valencia.

For a wild moment, I see a conspiracy here. The oranges that are grown in Andalucía are shipped to Valencia, while the oranges from Valencia are brought here and sold in Andalucía. It's a giant, make-work project that has already squeezed billions of euros out of other members of the European Union, especially the put-upon Germans. But I can tell that the man with the crates has no real interest in pursuing my theory, or, indeed, in having anything fur-ther to do with me. Fortunately, I can hear in the distance the clang-ing of a bell, which warns that the next service is about to begin.

"Must run," I tell the crate man. "Time for Sexta, so have to dash."

✠

Sexta proves to be a minor service with just three short psalms, a brief reading from the Bible, and a prayer—punctuated, in my case, by audible rumbles from my stomach, which had not been warned that yet another service would come between it and lunch.

At 1:30, we head back to the *hospedería* for *almuerzo*—the main meal of the day—where I remember to say grace and to down two large glasses of the much-promised, but sorely missed, *vino reserva*. The meal is a short one though, as we have to rush back to the church for the next *oficio* of Nona, which lasts a scant fifteen minutes. Rather than welcome its brevity, I find I'm irritated by the thought that it's too short a service to justify bringing a leisurely lunch to an end. I have time to settle into my pew—ready to savor the warmth of the church, the lulling repetition of the chanting, and the agreeable prospect of snoozing off the combined effects of the early-morning start and the two (or perhaps three) glasses of wine—when suddenly I'm expected to leave again.

Apparently, there is work to do—at least for the monks—who must man the laundry and the gift shop, and complete the other tasks that keep the business side of the monastery running. For those of us here as paying guests, we can read, study, wander the groves to watch the oranges ripen, or take a quick siesta.

And then it's time for Vespers, which is where we came in. We follow that with *cena*, and then Compline.

And so to bed—with the alarm once again set for 4:10 a.m.

☩

After several days, I realize I'm beginning to enjoy this. I like the routine, the repetition, with each day being exactly the same as the one before. I didn't think I'd be able to take it, I didn't think I could tolerate the stultifying boredom of prayer. But I find that I like the simplicity and the calmness that comes from a lack of choice.

In her book *The Bell Jar*, Sylvia Plath pictures herself trapped in the branches of a mature fig tree. She is surrounded by rich, fat, purple fruit—each fig symbolizing an opportunity in life that she knows is within her reach. But with so many options, she finds she is frozen into immobility—because if she chooses one fig, then she will have to give up the possibilities that all the others represent. So she stays in the tree, and watches as one by one the figs blacken and fall uneaten to the ground.

I never thought I would suffer from the same dilemma. It seems so overindulged—to be literally spoiled for choice. But these days it appears to be a common complaint, aggravated by the countless daily decisions we're forced to make. Walk into a typical supermarket and you'll find 50,000 varieties of items offered for sale. You may think, "I only want toothpaste," but if so, you will still have to select from among the nearly one hundred kinds you'll find stacked on the shelves—the same choice you'll face if you're just after shampoo or a basic household cleaner.

If you stop for coffee, where once you might have been asked, "black or white," "with or without sugar," you now must decide if you want tall, medium, short, caf, decaf, single-shot, double, triple, or quad, low-fat milk, no-fat milk, soy, organic, cappuccino, latte, gingerbread latte, cinnamon dolce latte, mocha, peppermint mocha twist, Americano, or skinny caramel macchiato. And that's just the espressos. If you want a muffin to go with it, you then have to mull over blueberry, bran, corn, chocolate chip, chocolate chunk, orange spice, pumpkin, lemon poppy seed, date, and walnut.

And so it goes. Which bank account, credit card, Internet provider, phone company, health plan, personal trainer, digital camera, electronic reader, tablet, personal music system, GPS, financial advisor, life coach, investment portfolio, retirement plan, airline to fly, movie to see, vacation to take, car to buy (or should that be lease). Scale that up to decisions that start to matter—where to live, who to marry, which job to take (if you can find one), and then move on to why are you here, what is the point, is there a God—and it's easy to see why many people, like Sylvia Plath, are frozen into immobility, suffering from an over-choice and need to decide, which leads not to greater satisfaction but to a kind of paralysis that's accompanied by a cocktail of negatives, including confusion, indecision, uncertainty, anxiety, and regret over roads not taken.

But not here in Las Escalonias. Not where every decision has already been made, and when every moment of every day has already been ordained.

Then, too, I'm beginning to like the chanting. I don't think I'm able to sing—even alone in the shower—but I can sustain a monotonous mumble that has the same tranquilizing effect as a mantra. It's hypnotic and relaxing, stilling my thoughts the way a hot toddy might soothe my body. Taking my mind away from itself and parking it in a neutral zone, where it can idle away with no particular place to go and no desire to get there.

What's happening, of course, is that I'm finding solace in the practice of religion, rather than in the underlying—and presumably necessary—faith. I'm even experiencing the camaraderie of belonging, in this case to a small group of people who rouse themselves in the middle of the night to chant, pray, and not make decisions. I tell myself that what I'm feeling is the attraction of cults—an abdication of responsibility that's common to the Hare Krishna movement, the Church of Scientology, or even, perhaps, the Manson Family. I have to tell myself this, because I'm starting to realize that the longer I stay here, the greater my chances of falling under a religious spell and remaining.

I'm finally saved one morning about ten minutes into Vigilia, which to my surprise has become my favorite service. I'm punch-drunk from a lack of sleep, but I find I can pass the time in a twilight state, cocooned in a benign setting where the outside world cannot get me.

During the psalms, my thoughts have not, I'm afraid, turned towards God but have instead drifted off in all directions, embarking on a meaningless journey of trivial discovery. I have learned, for example, that if I position my head just so and close my left eye, I can make the bell rope that hangs from the ceiling appear to cross the corner of one of the church windows; but if I close my right eye (I can't risk closing them both together or I'll fall completely asleep), then because of the parallax effect I can make the rope appear to cross the opposite corner of the window.

I'm sitting in my pew, quietly enjoying my rope-in-the-corner discovery, when suddenly the door of the church opens behind me and a young woman of about sixteen comes in, followed immediately by a man and then a couple of teenage boys. I assume they must be part of a family arriving late for the service, but then more people enter, boys and girls, girls and boys, until there are more than forty or fifty of them, streaming into the church and—as quietly as is possible for a pack of teenagers—filling all the rows of once-empty pews. The boys sit together, saving spaces for their friends, and the girls do the same. There's a lot of stifled giggling, the shuffling of feet, application of lipstick and mascara, as well as shoving and coughing. But the service proceeds without missing a beat.

When I get the chance, I quietly ask one of the girls why all these people are here in the middle of the night, and she whispers back that they're a party of schoolkids bussed in from Córdoba—here to sample a slice of monastic life to see if it might one day appeal to them. For me, the arrival of all these strangers has the opposite effect. It breaks the spell I've been falling under, and reminds me there's an outside world—one, I now realize, I would like to rejoin.

✠

We stick it out for three more days, attending the services but not moving noticeably closer to God. The monotony is alleviated by the weekend arrival of three new visitors, who join us in the *hospedería*. The first is a retired teacher who is now researching and writing a book about Andalucían folk songs. She's a regular here who is able to joke with Pepe and uncover the best of his sense of humor.

The other two are a couple, here for a long weekend. The man is a banker from Seville, about thirty-five years old. He sweeps in amid a flurry of excited activity. The other man is his partner, a shy good-looking hunk who stays more in the background. The banker is slender with black hair and gently sloping shoulders, while his companion is blond and muscled in a tight-fitting T-shirt that highlights the time he must spend in a gym. Both are excellent company—once I manage to overcome my deep-seated prejudice against bankers.

"I'm very, *very* devout," the banker confides to me over dinner. "So of course I believe in God. It's much better to believe than not to believe, don't you think?" As if faith is merely another one of those lifestyle choices—like deciding to live in Seville rather than move to Córdoba. "I think it would be very hard not to believe. I don't think I would like that at all."

He hands a walnut to his companion to crack.

"So could you ever become a monk?" I ask him.

The question elicits a peal of laughter. "Oh, no," he says, "I'm here just for the weekend and that's enough for me. I could never become a monk. My sexuality is much too important to me." He leans a little closer and lowers his voice. "What do you think the monks do about their sexuality? Perhaps because they are so old, their sexuality is not so important to them. But to me, my sexuality is so, so important I could never give it up. Maybe you could ask them. I don't have the nerve. Have you asked them about it yet? About their sexuality?"

"No," I tell him, "but I'll let Pepe know you were interested."

This elicits another peal of laughter—one that's a little nervy. He lightly places a hand on my arm "You wouldn't do *that*, would you? I could never, *ever* stay here again."

✛

The opportunity to ask the monks about their sexuality somehow never arises, but I do get the chance to talk to Pepe about his faith. The monks here have not been locked away in a cloister since they were too young to know anything else, so I'm hoping for some deeper answers to my perennial questions. As a former priest, Pepe has been out in the world, subject to the doubts and dissensions that must have assailed him (he did not take his vows until he was nearly forty), and his companions also have long secular pasts. The monk who plays the organ was a successful architect until he, too, was close to forty. And Brother Eugenio, the elevator monk, worked for Otis until well into advanced middle-age.

I settle down for a chat with Pepe on a sofa in the upstairs seating area of the *hospedería*. He's wearing a white habit, his legs crossed, with brown sensible shoes peeking out from underneath. The cell phone he habitually carries is clutched in one hand. He tells me again that he was a parish priest in Granada, but decided to become a monk—after long and careful thought—because he "wanted to get closer to God."

"I felt God pulling me. It was not enough just to be a priest. I wanted to get closer, and thought the best way to do that was to take the plunge and become a monk."

Does he ever doubt his decision? I ask.

He shakes his head. Any doubts he might have experienced were settled during the long process of becoming a monk. It's a drawn-out progression, he explains, so if you have any hesitation, then you don't take the final step. You don't commit to becoming a monk.

As he talks, I'm glad to see him stifle a yawn—something that all the monks do—so I ask him why the Liturgy of the Hours, the daily cycle of prayer, must start so early.

"We're talking to God," he says. "All the time we are talking to God. So we need an early start to keep the conversation going."

I'm not persuaded by this. It seems an unlikely God who would forget his creatures just because they went off the air for an hour or two longer. He concedes the point and admits there's another motive behind the middle-of-the-night start.

"Trappists belong to a strict Order. It's harder to worship God if we begin our prayers early. It would be much easier for us to stay in bed and start our prayers at, say, six or seven o'clock. But it would not be the same. So it's a small sacrifice we ask of ourselves, a sacrifice that brings us closer to God.

"Prayer," he adds, "is the central part of our lives. It's why we are here, to worship God and to recognize his presence. We are always focused on God, and we don't just pray in the church. We also pray in private, and we pray with and for other people, especially for the sick and infirm."

So are his prayers heard?

"Oh, yes. They are definitely heard. We know that because we have proof. We have testimonials from people who've been sick. They write to say that because of our prayers, they've now been cured."

"And that always happens?"

"No, not always. Sometimes they're cured and sometimes they aren't."

I tell him about a friend of mine who I know is religious. He is not a monk, but he prays a lot. I did not know how much until one day he told me that whenever he drives into a parking lot, he asks God to find him a space. "And do your prayers work?" I once asked him. "Sometimes they do," my friend told me. "And sometimes they don't."

Pepe shrugs at this little story but makes no direct response, so I ask him if he also prays for the big things in life—an end to wars, for example, and to disease and suffering.

"Oh, yes," he says again. "We pray for that, too."

But quite clearly those prayers are not being heard, I tell him. There's always a war somewhere.

"Yes, but we just offer our prayers up to God. We place them before him, but we have no power to make him grant what we ask for. That falls within the realm of God. It's up to him to decide whether or not he should act."

But suppose, I say, that God didn't exist. Wouldn't the result of his prayers be the same? Sometimes answered and sometimes not?

Pepe shrugs again. Perhaps, he says. But clearly the question is one he finds trite. Trappists—like all monks and nuns who are cloistered—do not feel the need to proselytize. So they don't try to persuade other people around to their way of thinking. It is enough for them to be secure in their faith—a faith, Pepe says, that is just *there*.

"It doesn't matter where it comes from or how you get it. It's either inside you or it isn't. You can say it comes from God or you can say it comes from within. But if it's there inside you, you will find it."

I tell him I envy him his beliefs, since so many studies have shown that people with faith are considerably happier than those without. If you don't have faith, you don't have the off-the-rack religion that usually comes with it, a religion that governs your thoughts and behavior; nor do you have the security that comes from joining a community of like-minded people. So you have to construct a bespoke philosophy and morality of your own, and find purpose and meaning somewhere else.

"Life," I tell him, "would be much easier if I had faith."

He looks at me for a long moment.

"You think," he says finally, "that the life of a monk is *easy?*"

✠

On our last day, as we nose the Panda back down the Tara drive-way to rejoin the world, I realize I've developed a high level of respect for the monks and nuns we've met on this journey. At the outset, I had an unconscious tendency to view them as oddi-ties—an interesting but anachronistic group of people who were out of touch and no longer relevant in a modern world. But now I see the full extent of their commitment.

I'm quite sure I'll never join them (assuming they might one day want me)—and equally certain I'll never be able to share their beliefs. Knowledge tells me that religion is a result of natu-ral selection—it helped individuals survive by making them part of mutually supportive and structured groups—and it was an easy sell since it allowed people to think they could cheat death. Also, my Occam's razor reasoning says there's no need to postulate God, as the world would look the same, even if he didn't exist. Then, too, I lack the ego to assume that a deity who created the Universe can really take an interest in me, no matter how much I want to stop a war, recover from an illness, or even find an empty space in a parking lot.

I still believe that having a religion, having a faith, is an important ingredient of personal happiness. But having seen close up how monks and nuns live, I'm not so sure that their version of personal happiness doesn't come with too high a price.

When I look back on the long course of human history, then—like anyone else—I tend to highlight the key events that have shaped our development. The discovery of fire. The cultivation of wheat. The rise of city states and empires. I might also include the development of writing, the invention of zero, the scientific and industrial revolutions, and maybe the advent of the computer and the growth of the Internet. There would be no end to the list. But if I believed—*truly* believed, like Pepe does—that at some point in our relatively recent past, the God I believed in sent his only Son to Earth to save me, then no matter the key event I chose to highlight, it would pale into nothing and become merely a blip when set against this monumental spike of GOD ARRIVING HERE ON EARTH. Under those circumstances, I like to think that I, too, would be compelled to build my entire life around that one spectacular manifestation.

Many people profess to believe, and no doubt most of them feel they genuinely do. Yet very few people commit themselves totally the way Pepe has done. He may enjoy the rewards of faith—the happiness and certainty that goes along with it. But to my mind he has also chosen to shoulder a heavy and wearisome burden.

Convento de la Purísima Concepción
(Santa María) Marchena

✠

Franciscan-Clarissa

{FOURTEEN}

WE HAVE ONE MORE MONASTERY TO VISIT TO BRIDGE THE SHORT gap between Las Escalonias and our final destination of Málaga on the Costa del Sol and the southern Mediterranean coast. In this part of Spain—the former Muslim stronghold—there are fewer monasteries for us to choose from than in the northern, mostly Christian part. But there are still more than enough to provide us with a reasonable selection.

We look first at the Convento Inmaculada Concepción, in the attractive spa town of Alhama southwest of Granada, but we're told by the resident nun who answers our phone call that the monastery is closed to visitors, mainly because it's in danger of collapsing as it no longer has funds for repairs. So we settle instead on the Convento de la Purísima Concepción (Santa María) in the town of Marchena, about forty miles east of Seville.

After Las Escalonias, we look forward to staying in the middle of a town near the urban facilities—bars and cafes, cafes and bars—that we have been missing. With a population of about twenty thousand, Marchena is small enough to be manageable, but big enough to offer some kind of nightlife. Also, it's well positioned for easy side trips to the Roman ruins in Carmona, the eighteenth-century mansions of Écija, and the neighboring towns of Osuna and Estepa.

If you're any way inclined to follow in the footprints of the dead and the famous, these latter two towns will appeal, because they are both stops on the Washington Irving Route that runs from Seville to Granada. This route—another one of those manufactured itineraries dreamt up by worthy organizations (in this case, an Andalucían historical society) to lure visitors into a particular area—is meant to commemorate a journey that Irving, the nineteenth-century American writer and diplomat, made through Andalucía before arriving in the then-abandoned Alhambra and penning a best-selling book of short stories. His *Tales of the Alhambra* is credited with turning a generation of Americans into Spanish tourists eager to experience the unique and foreign romanticism of Muslim Spain. With its stories of princesses, castles, ghosts, and gardens, it still has the power to do that today.

With this kind of day-tripping in mind, we shamelessly plan to treat the Marchena monastery like a hotel—not something we would normally do, and not something we would usually recommend. But we've done enough scouting ahead to discover that the Franciscan Clarissa nuns in the *convento* have no problem with that. On the contrary, their website—like a number of monasteries these days, it's fully online—specifically promotes the monastery's location and the access it gives to interesting towns nearby.

This is an attraction that definitely appeals, as we have no plans to attend any more services, but will instead revert to type and have some simple vacation fun. Furthermore, we already know what the occupants of the monastery are most likely to be—devout, bespectacled, and rapidly dwindling in numbers.

As it turns out, we couldn't have been more wrong.

✠

The last of the daylight is beginning to fade as we drive into Marchena, but since we've been told that the monastery we're looking for is both in the center of town and perched high on a hill, we're confident we'll find it even in the dark. That belief might have held up in the seventeenth century when La Purísima Concepción (Santa María) was founded, and it may well be valid for Marchena locals who have grown up navigating the twists and turns of their one-way streets and dead-end alleys. But it is not true for us. We can see the promised hill as well as a church tower (that must belong to the monastery) peeking coyly over the tiled roofs around it, but to get from here to there is beyond our navigational skills.

We're forced to abandon the Panda and continue our search on foot, zigzagging upwards on slick cobbled streets until finally we reach a Muslim-era arch that marks the entrance to a narrow passageway that in turn leads to a rough track that seems to go even higher up the hill. We hike up it and a few minutes later emerge into an expansive area, the size of a football field, right at the summit. It's a military parade ground, or so it would seem—sandy and barren except for a few palm trees that struggle for life along one side. At its center, there's a long row of tidily parked cars, while immediately opposite stand the high walls of the *convento*.

We retrace our steps to retrieve the Panda, easing it through the Muslim-era arch, its wing mirrors snapped in to avoid scraping the walls, and park neatly alongside the other cars. Then we start the long walk across the parade ground to the monastery entrance. The first thing I notice is that the church whose tower we earlier spotted has a twin brother that's been built right next to it, so close that the two of them are almost touching. Two churches seems a little excessive even for a mon-astery—like wearing a belt as well as suspenders—but on closer inspection I see that one of the churches is accessible from the parade ground while the other can be reached only from inside the monastery walls.

The church in the parade ground looks permanently closed—perhaps because of the dangerous state of its scoliotic tower—but when we step through a nearby gate and into the monastery-proper, we find the second church booming with life. So much sound is coming from it that its walls and roof should be pulsating as if in an animated cartoon. The sound is not from an organ, nor from a congregation joined together in a song of praise, but is instead the driving beat of drums. If I were not looking right at it, I would swear I was standing outside a basement nightclub. There is clearly no requirement for *silencio* here.

We ring the bell by the iron-grilled gate, but of course there's no answer. Everyone is inside the church. We follow the alley to our right towards the church and ease open a side door. We're blown back by the roar of the drums, which rises to a whole new level, and as we take a tentative step inside the church a barrage of flashlights explodes in our eyes. This is not a surprise party in our honor; the flashes come from digital cameras aimed at the altar, where three rows of nuns are shimmying in their habits, swinging and swaying in time to the music like a 1960s' all-girl pop group. All the nuns are young. They're also African black.

The congregation, too, is moving in time, like acidheads at a rock concert. Most have abandoned their pews and are on their feet in the aisles, clapping their hands above their heads and reeling and rocking with the rhythm. Many of the revelers are nuns— also young, also black, and also dressed in their habits. The rest are short, squat, middle-aged, and white. One—an elderly man who should probably know better—is standing precariously on the seat of a pew, a camcorder rolling in his hands, while others jostle one another like paparazzi as they try to get the best shot of the swinging nuns at the altar.

We've timed our arrival badly—or perhaps we've timed it well. Either way, as we push our way farther into the church, the beat of the drums reaches a crescendo and abruptly comes to an end. The service—if that's what it was—is over. There's a burst of prolonged and unseemly applause, then the congregation moves en masse towards the door we just came through. The dancing nuns jump down from their impromptu stage near the altar and merge into the crowd. They're all about twenty years old—fresh-faced with silky complexions and big grins. One of them detaches herself from the group and elbows her way towards us, waving a welcome with open palms.

"I can tell you're not Spanish," she says in perfect Americanized English.

"And nor are you."

She laughs. "No. From Kenya," she says, and points at the other young nuns—aspirants, really—who have formed a semi-circle around us. "This one's from Uganda, she's from Madagascar, this one's from Tanzania, and the others are, like me, from Kenya."

Everything about these nuns is completely at odds with their sober habits and veils. They could be schoolgirls at a fair who, for a laugh, have poked their faces through cardboard cutouts so they can be photographed looking like nuns. One of them leans forward and exudes a freshly laundered smell as she gives me a kiss on each cheek. There are six of them gathered around us, and, they tell us, they've been in Spain for only a matter of days. They are, they say, aspiring novices who, this evening, are being inducted into the Clarissa Order—an Order that is normally cloistered. But not, apparently, today.

"Wow," one of them says, looking around at the crowd. "Oh, wow. Isn't this amazing?"

Ten minutes later I'm inside the monastery's *comedor*—the dining room attached to the *hospedería*—with a beer in one hand and tapas in the other. The nuns are throwing a party to celebrate their entry into the Clarissa community. They are not allowed to

attend the party themselves, but they've laid on a buffet of cana-
pés, sandwiches, cold meats, potato croquettes, almonds, olives,
and trays and trays of homemade marzipan cakes and cookies—in
addition to a well-stocked bar. We are now being treated as fully
paid-up members of the congregation that was in the church—
town folk from Marchena who have come here to help the Order
celebrate the newly recruited nuns from Africa—and apparently
we have arrived on one of the rare occasions when the nuns are
allowed to mingle freely with them.

The elderly photographer who was wobbling on a pew is still
recording, shooting scenes with his camcorder of equally elderly
matrons who are standing around in sensible clothes, chugging
Cruzcampo beer straight from the bottle.

"This is quite a party," one of them says, and, like me, helps
herself to another drink.

When the celebrations start to wind down, we leave the
comedor and try to check into our cell. We again ring the bell
by the iron-grilled gate and this time get buzzed into a cupboard
of a room with a wooden *torno*—like the one in El Toboso—set
into the far wall. Two Spanish matrons who were at the party
squeeze in beside us—not to book a room (we're once again the
only people staying here), but to buy more of the marzipan sweets
that were served at the buffet. We're wedged together, intimately
close, in a space that's smaller than a European elevator.

The Spanish matrons can't decide which sweets they want
to buy. There's a long menu pinned to the wall that lists the
wide variety of shapes, sizes, and boxes. As they argue over their

choice, we maneuver around them and push another bell by the *torno*. We know the routine by now. The nuns are back in their quarters, and while they may have been kissing us in church, they will now be secluded, barricaded inside their cloister so they cannot see—or be seen by—us. When we hear a shuffle of feet and the murmur of voices on the other side of the *torno*, we shout through the wooden barrier that hides them to say that we've booked a room.

There's a rustle of papers, then the word "Passports" is barked out like a military command.

I place our passports on the turntable base of the *torno* and give it half a spin. The *torno* revolves and the passports disappear. A few minutes later, the *torno* again swivels round and we're presented with a registration card that we need to complete, as well as two sets of keys.

"Room Seven," the voice says. "Forty-six euros a night."

✠

We cross a pebbled courtyard decorated with potted plants, a central fountain, and a small marble statue of the Virgin, then climb the stairs of the *hospedería* to find our room. A lone lizard freezes on the wall above us, playing dead as we pass him by.

Room Seven turns out to be the best cell we have stayed in. It's cool, spotlessly clean, and furnished with two single beds, a desk, and a comfortable armchair. There's even a TV in case we want to watch Real Madrid defeat yet another of its rivals. Since the nuns here earn a large part of their living by taking in laundry—when they're not making marzipan sweets and cakes—there is a ready supply of freshly pressed sheets for the beds and pristine towels in the bathroom. Hot water arrives at the showerhead at the mere twitch of the faucet, and hotel-room extras—such as tissues and miniature shampoos—are once again available.

There are, of course, some quirks. It's required that we vacate the room between noon and 1:00 p.m. since that's when the nuns have time between their prayers to come in to clean, and it would, apparently, be a calamity if we were ever to see them. Then, too, the lighting on the stairs is on an economical rapid-fire timer that switches off within seconds, plunging us into the dark if we come in at night, and it switches on again only in response to vigorous motion, forcing us to stop every few minutes to perform rigorous sets of boot-camp star jumps.

More annoyingly, we soon discover that there are four active churches within earshot of the *hospedería*. This wouldn't matter, but for the fact that each of the churches chimes out the hours; and their clocks are not synchronized. At one o'clock that's not a problem, but if you're dropping off to sleep right around midnight, it's disconcerting to hear that the time is an Alice-in-Wonderland forty-eight o'clock.

Still, from our window we have a sweeping panorama that takes in much of Marchena's long history. The military parade ground where we parked was once the site of a Muslim fort, or *alcazár*, as well as a mosque. Later, after Marchena was reclaimed by Christendom—in 1240 (by a Ferdinand, damn it, not an

Alphonso)—the area became the site of a palace built by the fourth Duke of Arcos, an aristocratic bigwig whose family was honored with a large gift of land in Marchena. He founded the monastery here in 1624, then moved it inside his palace walls in 1631.

The row of palm trees we saw on the way in is all that remains of the duke's palace gardens. The palace itself has disappeared, along with the Muslim fort; they've been replaced by a few squat whitewashed houses and, I suspect, by the *hospedería* where we are staying. As for the mosque that once stood here, it's been reborn as the church of Santa María de la Mota—that is, as the now-boarded-up church that stands in the corner of the parade ground.

✠

For the next several days, we explore Marchena and its bars and restaurants, which keep us comfortably watered and fed. We also exploit Marchena's location, which, as the monastery's website promises, places it at the heart of a spider's web of roads that lead to towns with tangled Roman, Muslim, Christian, and Spanish aristocratic pasts. On successive days, it's relatively easy to visit Córdoba, Seville, Cádiz, Gibraltar, Marbella, and even Granada, but we settle for towns that are nearer. They are as ripe with history as any of those that are farther away—although it's not always easy to understand that history when you pay them a visit.

In Écija, for example, we poke our noses into some of the grand mansions that the local gentry built during the eighteenth century, but when we pick up a brochure—put out by the town's tourist board—to find out more about them, we are told only that "the development of the landholder property has designate all the posterior history." And when we move on to Carmona—a once-Roman town with a large necropolis—we are told by a plaque in a museum, "For the rites it was transcendental and in testaments there were sometimes specific instructions to the heirs for their celebration." I am still mulling this over when the next plaque tells me, "In death there are not only but classes"—a contention that may have been true in Roman times, but surely not one you'd want to defend today.

Back in Marchena, the information flow begins to improve when we dip into the sacristy of the fourteenth-century Mudéjar parish church of San Juan Bautista to see nine major works by Francisco Zurbarán, the seventeenth-century Spanish artist. The church venerates John the Baptist, who, of course, suffered death by decapitation. That should be easy enough to explain, but in the English translation of their plaque by the door, the local authorities designate the building as The Slitting Throat Church of John the Baptist.

{FIFTEEN}

CHRISTIAN MONASTERIES MAY HAVE BEEN ESTABLISHED IN EUROPE during the sixth century, but in Egypt their origins can be traced from the late third or early fourth century, when a few stalwart aesthetics who had set themselves up alone in caves in the desert decided to band together into a community. With a history going back that far, it might seem rash—even impertinent—to question their future, but clearly attracting new blood is a serious challenge that vexes all monasteries in Europe today. Many rely passively on would-be novitiates hearing the call of God and then turning up on their doorsteps, but others are more proactive, employing a wide range of marketing techniques that first get people's attention and then lure the would-be apprentices into their Orders.

When we explored the town of Écija, we tried to get into its Barefoot Carmelite monastery of San José, since it's housed in a fourteenth-century former Mudéjar palace. But the nuns there—there are only a handful of them left—are adamant: No visitors of any kind. They are willing to speak to visitors, but they do not go out themselves, and they do not allow the outside world to come in to them. At the tourist office in town, we learned that this attitude has put them at odds with the local government, which wants to open San José up and charge passing tourists for the privilege of looking inside this historic palace. The government is sure it will soon prevail, because most of the nuns are well past their allotted time of three score years and ten; and when they all pass on, the government thinks it'll be able to move in and take control.

The nuns, however, are fighting back. If they can attract new recruits, they'll be able to keep the monastery within their Order. That's not an easy task if you're tightly cloistered, but the Écija nuns—in spite of their age and lack of worldly savvy—have come up with a twenty-first-century solution and launched their own video on YouTube. It's a professional job, as skilled as any corporate recruitment video you're likely to see at a jobs fair. Atmospheric music plays in the background as soft-sell pictures of monastic lifestyle float slowly across the viewer's screen. Nuns are shown sewing and baking, tending to plants in the monastery's patio, and sitting in comfortable surroundings while quietly reading. They're also shown talking to a person from the outside world—from behind the safety of a grille, of course.

The images are overlaid with religious messages in large type, and the final screen gives potential recruits the monastery's address, phone number, and e-mail. When last checked, the San José video had received some 165,000 views, and at least one prospective novice has shown up at the door and been welcomed into the community.

Here in Marchena, the Clarissa Order has faced a similar problem. Fifteen years ago, it could field just six nuns in its monastery here—all of them elderly. Like their San José sisters, the Santa María nuns were able to read the writing on the wall. And they knew, too, that their monastery was under threat—not from a government body but from the aristocratic heirs of the fourth Duke of Arcos, the local bigwig whose palace once stood on these grounds. These heirs are, apparently, the true owners of the monastery. The nuns just have title to live here, and they will forfeit that right if there are no nuns left alive to occupy the buildings. With this threat hanging over it, the Order set out to attract new members, turning its attention overseas and actively recruiting in Africa.

We get the lowdown on this situation when we meet the Abbess who's in charge of Santa María. We can't just drop in on her, of course, so we arrange to meet her in the *locutorium*—part of the inner sanctum that we reach only after we shout for the key through the wooden barrier of the *torno*, and then let ourselves in at the appointed time.

The Abbess is already there, gripping the bars of the grille that divides the *locutorium* into two neighboring cages. In the gloom, all we can initially see are the whites of her eyes, the white of her wimple, and the mile-wide smile of her bleach-white teeth, hanging in the air like the Cheshire Cat's grin. As our eyes adjust to the darkness, we see she cuts a statuesque figure, and we quickly learn that she's every bit as jolly as she looks. Her conversation is punctuated by belly-shaking laughs, and even when she tries to be serious, the Abbess appears on the point of chortling at some inner joke. Right away, it's impossible not to warm to her.

On the faithless side of the grille, we pull up chairs to a glass-topped table embellished with a broad swatch of presumably home-crocheted lace. On the walls around us the saints are back, staring glumly down from their paintings or gazing mournfully up at the sky. Next to the grille a sign reminds us—lest we've forgotten—that, *Mi vivir es Cristo*. My life is Christ.

The Abbess—aka Sister Susannah—lets go of the bars and settles into a comfortable chair on her side of the grille. She was born in Kenya, she tells us, in a town called Machakos, which is about forty miles from the capital of Nairobi. Growing up, she had no intention of becoming a nun, although she was involved in "active community work like helping the poor and caring for the sick." However, about fifteen years ago, when she was twenty, she was recruited by the Clarissa Order and flown here to the monastery in Marchena, where, she says, she expected to perform similar work, perhaps becoming a nurse.

"I was uncomfortable at first," she says, "because of the strange food, the foreign language, and the different climate. Also, I was young and there were only six other nuns here. And all of them were old."

Nevertheless, she stayed, adjusted, and now she has no plans to leave. In the past fifteen years, she has been back to Kenya to visit her family only twice; but she is not homesick because her real-life sister has also come from Kenya and is now part of the Clarissa Order, too. The six other nuns who used to be here have been reduced to two—both Spanish, both white, and both about eighty years old. They would constitute the entire community were it not for the Clarissa recruitment in Africa, which has now boosted the number of nuns to twenty-one.

Most of the new arrivals come from Kenya, where many of the monasteries are full. But the Clarissas have reached into other countries, too—mainly Tanzania and Uganda. The Order pays to fly the recruits to Marchena, and pays for—and organizes—the special visas needed by the nuns so they can legally enter Spain. Quite what the Order says to the aspirant nuns is hard to say. But of the six whose initiation party we gate-crashed, one has already returned home, having quickly learned that life here was not for her.

When Sister Susannah first came here, the Clarissas neglected to mention the fact that the monastery she was joining happened to be cloistered. So instead of venturing into the community to tend to the poor and the sick, Sister Susannah was expected to spend the rest of her days sequestered indoors with access to the outside world filtered through the bars of a cage.

So how did she react when she learned the truth?

Sister Susannah lets fly with one of her belly laughs. "With a big 'Wow!'" she says. "A *very* big 'Wow!'"

✠

Like all monastery heads, Sister Susannah has been elected to her post by a majority of her charges—in her case, the nuns who now fall under her care. If they approve, she can be elected to more than one term and serve for a total of twelve consecutive years or even longer, if she's able to obtain special permission from Rome. As the head honcho, she is expected to follow the rules of her Order, so, for example, she has to ensure that the Liturgy of the Hours—the seven services spread throughout the day—is properly followed. But she is also able to exercise a considerable amount of discretion.

That leeway only becomes apparent when we ask her about her daily routine and the way she handles the monastery's affairs.

She begins by saying that in spite of her boisterous nature and thwarted ambition to become a nurse, she enjoys "the contemplative life."

"It doesn't mean I hide away in a monastery and avoid all problems. Instead it means I've developed an inner peace, an inner happiness that I wouldn't otherwise possess. I listen to God—not with my ears but with my being. I don't know why, but that just makes me feel good inside."

So she doesn't miss the life she would have led in Kenya?

"Jesus made a sacrifice for us," she says, "so it's only right that we make a sacrifice for him. I won't get married. I won't have children. But that doesn't bother me, because all the children in the world are mine. It's an honor to serve Jesus, so I don't really feel I'm making a sacrifice. We have to continue to carry his cross. That's what I want to do, so I'm happy to stay here. I will be here until I die. I will stay in this place forever."

She tells us, when we ask, that the monastery once had many benefactors who helped it out financially. "But not anymore," she says. "We get no help from the government, so now we are on our own."

As well as doing the laundry, running the *hospedería,* and baking and selling marzipan sweets, the nuns offer three meals a day in the *comedor.* They also sell ice cream in the summer when the market for marzipan falls off, they produce and sell lace and cloths that they embroider themselves, and they maintain on the side a small "farm" of rabbits, cockerels, and ducks.

"There's always a lot of work to do," Sister Susannah says.

Only when we ask her to run through a typical day and she mentions "a period of entertainment" do we begin to realize that there might be a less serious side to this monastery's life. We have already noticed that although Santa María is nominally cloistered, there is an unusual amount of interaction with the outside world. The nuns make frequent forays into Marchena—driving their own car when they go shopping—and they often play host to a steady stream of non-Church visitors. In some of the other monasteries we've stayed in, I've sometimes felt the need to tiptoe around and speak only in whispers. But I don't feel that here.

At first, Sister Susannah is hesitant to elaborate on her "period of entertainment," but then she admits that it sometimes involves "watching videos."

"Is that all?" I ask.

"Yes, that's all," she says, although her belly laugh contradicts the nod of her head. "Well, perhaps," she adds, "we might do a little comedy."

"Oh?"

"Yes. We sometime tell jokes," and she releases another of her laughs just at the thought of them. "And no, they're not always religious."

"So what else do you do?"

"Well, we might play some music. Maybe even dance."

Dancing nuns? Telling jokes? "But you don't have any partners," I say.

"No, that's true." And now she is nearly doubled up with laughter. "So we have to make do with what we've got. We have to improvise. So some of us dress up and act like men. We can't always be serious," she says. "Not all of the time. We still have to live."

☩

The day we leave Marchena we pack up the Panda for our drive to Málaga, our final destination on the Mediterranean coast, where we plan to drop off the car and fly home. The thought of Málaga doesn't appeal. Overbuilt and overrun with cars, it is the main transport hub for the Costa del Sol as well as a key entry point for those sixty-or-so million tourists who visit the country each year—the tourists that on this trip we have managed to avoid.

Before we drive away from the monastery, we ring the bell by the gate and get buzzed into the cupboard that houses the *torno*. We've already paid our bill and retrieved our passports, but I want to return our two sets of keys and say goodbye. I can hear muffled voices on the other side of the *torno*, so I know there are at least two nuns there.

"Returning our keys," I shout at the wooden barrier between us.

I put the keys on the turntable-base of the *torno* and give it a spin and the keys disappear. I'm not expecting anything in return, so I am not surprised when the torno stops after half a turn. But then it starts to revolve again, making another half-turn and delivering back to me three large boxes of marzipan sweets.

"Take these," a muffled voice shouts. "For your journey. A gift from us for you to enjoy. The sweets will go with you. And God will go with you, too."

How to Plan Your Own Trip

THIS BOOK MAINLY TELLS THE STORY OF A JOURNEY THAT WE TOOK, but we hope you will turn it around and see it also as an indication of the kinds of experiences you would enjoy if you were to make a similar trip through Spain, staying only in monasteries. You might not meet nuns who dress up as men, kiss you on the cheek, and offer you a beer, and you might not stumble upon a library of antiquarian books, a sawn-in-half Baroque *retablo*, or a priceless Flemish masterpiece that should, perhaps, be hanging in Belgium's Royal Museum of Fine Arts. But you will undoubtedly encounter something equally arresting and bizarre, which, figuratively speaking, hits you over the head and permanently lodges in your memory, because it is so unexpected and off the wall.

The daily routine of monastic life may appear fixed and repetitive, conforming to the Liturgy of the Hours; and the layout of nearly all monasteries may appear to follow the same general pattern of a central cloister surrounded by a chapter room, refectory, dormitory, and church. But every monastic experience is fundamentally different from every other, and that—more than anything else—is what, in our opinion, makes staying in monasteries so endlessly rewarding. You never know what will come next. You never know who you will meet. Yet all you need to enjoy the experience is an open mind and a flexible attitude (and possibly a sense of humor, too).

If you like the idea of traveling through Spain and staying in ancient monasteries, here's what we suggest you do:

CHOOSE A ROUTE

First, pick a route. Spain has so many monasteries that no matter where you go, you're sure to find ones you can stay in. So start with your journey, rather than with the monasteries themselves. We planned our route so we could travel from Christian Spain to Muslim Spain. We wanted to see some of the legacies of the Muslim conquest that survive in the buildings, food, and customs. We also thought these Muslim bequests would contrast well with the Christian monasteries we planned to stay in and use as bases. The monasteries we chose allowed us to do this. They also allowed us to visit some of Spain's most spectacular cities—Barcelona, Zaragoza, Pamplona, Segovia, Ávila, Toledo, Córdoba, Seville, and Granada—while letting us explore many of the smaller towns and villages that most visitors ignore.

SET CRITERIA

Second, decide on the kinds of monasteries you want to stay in. Again, there are enough to choose from, so you can take your pick. In addition to giving us access to the cities listed above, we selected our monasteries on the basis of three main criteria. First, the monastery had to house a functioning religious community with at least a skeleton crew of monks or nuns on-site (it could not be a tourist mecca or an upscale hotel-*parador* that had lost its religious function). Second, it had to offer us the chance to mingle with this religious community (since part of the appeal of monasteries is that they allow you to get to know how the residents live). And third, the monastery had to offer accommodations to both men and women (although not necessarily in the same room or in the same part of the building).

IDENTIFY THE MONASTERIES

Begin with the Internet. It's by far the best source for finding monasteries you might want to stay in. We used the website www.guiasmonasterios.com, which lists many of the monasteries in Spain (as of this writing, there is no website that lists all of the monasteries). This site is divided by region, so click on the regions you're planning to visit. The lists of monasteries that then appear will be in Spanish, so you might want to have a Spanish-English dictionary in hand. But if you're looking for monasteries with accommodations you can stay in (rather than ones you can just visit), you need only search the listings for the words *hospedería*, *hospedaje*, and *residencia*—the three interchangeable words that describe a monastic lodging—or for the word *habitaciónes*, which means "rooms." We found El Real Monasterio de Santo Tomás in Ávila on this site, as well as El Monasterio de la Santa María de las Escalonias near Córdoba.

Another website we found useful is www.top-tour-of-Spain .com, which surprisingly, given its package-tour-sounding name, has about twenty worthwhile monastic listings. We discovered the cloistered El Reial Monestir de Santa María de Vallbona and the more open (with restaurant and bar) El Monasterio de la Virgen de Monlora on this site. To see the monasteries the site lists, click on "Site Map," scroll down to "Travel" and click on that, then scroll down until you find the subheading "Hotel Information for Spain." Under this subheading, you will see another sub-subheading called "Monastery Hotels in Spain" (a bit of a misnomer), which will yield the listings.

You can also get in touch with the Spanish General Office of Tourism. As far as we know, it has no online information about still-occupied monasteries you can stay in, but it has compiled a list of about seventy monasteries that accept paying guests— including those that only admit people on spiritual retreat or undertaking religious studies. To obtain this list, e-mail the office at infosmile@tourspain.es.

As an alternative, you can, of course, simply search online for suitable monasteries by inputting the word "monasteries" (or *monasterios*) along with the town or region you would like to visit—e.g., "monasteries in León Spain"—but this approach is hit-and-miss and as likely as not will yield monasteries that are now *paradors* or ones you can visit but cannot stay in.

If you prefer to consult something called a "book," you might want to try *Lodging in Spain's Monasteries*, by Eileen Barish. It gives descriptions of monasteries and outlines the facilities and services they offer; it also has contact details and information on nearby towns. The book was published in 2002, which might make it appear out of date, but monasteries don't change much (although their policies towards paying guests can change unpredictably).

REFINE YOUR SEARCH
Once you've identified the monasteries you might want to stay in, you should go to their individual websites. A surprising number of monasteries are online, with sophisticated sites, easily searched for, that will give you all the information you need.

MAKE A BOOKING
It's not a good idea to turn up at a monastery unless you have a reservation. You might find that the *hospedería* is filled with a group on retreat—or (just as likely) that the resident monks or nuns have decided to shut their lodgings down for a while. Most monasteries have a system of some kind that allows you to book, but each monastery's requirements are different. If a monastery has a website, it will usually accept an e-mail booking. When we tried to reserve this way, we always received a response—but not necessarily right away.

If you prefer to book by phone, try to call between 10:00 a.m. and noon (Spanish time)—that's after Terce and before Sexta, when you're more likely to catch someone in between prayers. Expect to wait for many rings before the phone is answered. Monasteries do not employ receptionists. Also, they're big places. A monk or nun may have a long walk to get to the phone and won't want to be rushed, especially if he/she is seventy-five years old. When the phone is answered, you might have to shout.

That said, some of the monks and nuns we met—especially those charged specifically with administering a *hospedería*—walked around with a cell phone in hand, so were always instantly contactable (and helpful). If you reserve by phone, you might still be asked to send a confirming e-mail. You might also be asked for a credit card number, but most likely you'll just be told "We look forward to seeing you when you arrive."

THE LANGUAGE PROBLEM

If you plan to reserve by phone, you will need a passing acquaintance with Spanish, since you cannot rely on the person who answers your call being fluent in English. Fortunately, the Spanish people (unlike, say, the French) are not offended if you butcher their language, so you can barrel ahead without being ridiculed or rude. The "Making a Hotel Reservation" section in any Spanish phrase book will tell you the words you need to use.

If you're writing an e-mail, you can always compose it in English and then use a service like Bing Translator (at www.bingtranslator.com) to turn it into Spanish. The response you receive from the monastery can also be translated this way if it doesn't immediately make sense to you. Key words to look for are *libre*, meaning there's a room free; *completo*, meaning "nope, we're full"; *habitación*, meaning "a room"; *doble*, meaning "double"; *con baño*, meaning "bathroom en suite"; and *tarifa*, meaning "price."

Regardless of how you make your booking, the rate will be quoted to you in euros. Sometimes breakfast will be included, but more often not. Sometimes there's no charge at all for the room—as we found at El Monasterio de la Virgen de Monlora—but you will then most likely be asked to make a donation. The amount you give is entirely up to you.

WHAT TO EXPECT WHEN YOU ARRIVE

Expect to get lost. A lot of Spanish monasteries were built in hard-to-reach places that are not served by public transport, so if you're staying in one of those, you will need a car and a map or GPS. In cities, the monasteries should be easier to find, but in fact they are not. They are usually close to the center of a town that grew up around them over the course of many centuries—which means they're probably surrounded by a rat run of streets that are narrow, one-way, and deliberately confusing. On the plus side, the monastery itself is bound to be large and so hard to disguise. But don't expect the locals to know where it is. There's not much interaction between even the most prominent of monasteries and the city or town that surrounds it.

WHAT TO WEAR

It's probably a good idea to leave the Gucci bags and Jimmy Choo shoes at home, since they're likely to be out of place in an establishment that embraces poverty. Modest and respectful attire is best: long pants, not shorts, and nothing revealing or tight. If you have to accessorize, do so with a flashlight—handy for lighting your way to those predawn services and for finding the route back to your room.

Instead of style, think about warmth. Even in summer, the rooms, corridors, and chapels can be cold, and at other times of the year they can be downright freezing. There may be heating, but to economize, many monasteries turn it off until the resident monks or nuns are ready for bed—and even then, it is only turned on long enough to take the chill off the cells. You won't need woolly pajamas, but you will need a fleece.

CHECKING IN
This can take time. Most monasteries do not have a reception desk or anything equivalent. Instead, somewhere near the entrance, either on the wall outside or just beyond the main doors, there will be a bell you can press (it might be marked *portería*), and after several minutes—as many as five or ten—a monk or nun will arrive to greet you. Of course, if you turn up at the monastery when the residents are at prayer, you can ring the bell as much as you like and still get no response. So it's a good idea to have a general idea of the times of the Liturgy of the Hours and plan your arrival accordingly.

Once you've established face-to-face contact, you can try out your Spanish and say that you have a reservation for a room. Monks and nuns are remarkably patient if you have only basic language skills—or no skills at all. After all, they've often been there fifty years, with no plans to go elsewhere. Alternatively, you can simply find an appropriate sentence in a Spanish phrase book and show them that. Remember, too, that you're likely to be the only foreigner trying to check in on that day, so the monk/nun will have a pretty good idea of who you are and why you've just rung the bell.

YOUR ROOM (OR CELL)

Most cells in monastic *hospederías* cost considerably less than rooms in tourist hotels. Standards sometimes reflect this. However, it's not possible to predict the standard of accommodation since it can vary so much. But in our experience, all rooms will be spotlessly clean. They'll have everything you need, but no frills. Most will have an en suite bathroom with shower, toilet, and sink. And because so many monasteries take in laundry to generate income, the sheets and towels will be freshly washed and immaculately ironed. That last luxury aside, it's best to think "small and simple"—that way, you're less likely to feel disappointed.

FOOD AND DRINK

The quality of the meals also can vary widely—from none at all to delicious homegrown produce that's served with a full-bodied homemade wine. If you're staying in a monastery that's relatively remote, it's a good idea to have your own supplies—just in case. Some bread, fruit, and cheese will do, as well as, perhaps, a bottle or two of Spanish red, which never seems to go amiss. In monasteries where the meals are provided, you're expected to eat when the community does—although not necessarily in the same room or at the same table.

Some monasteries include meals in the price of the accommodation—often because there's nowhere else in the vicinity for you to eat. Most, however, allow you to elect which, if any, meals you would like. If you decide to eat in, breakfast will likely consist of bread, butter and jam, coffee or tea, and perhaps some fruit or juice. Lunch—served late at around 2:00 p.m.—is the main meal of the day, and will probably be soup; pasta or meat and potatoes; salad; fruit or yogurt; and a glass (two if you're fast) of red wine. Dinner—also served late at around 8:30 p.m. (early by Spanish standards)—is a more simple affair, often just an omelet with cured meat, a salad, and bread and fruit.

Don't forget to stand to say grace before you sit to eat. And in some monasteries, be prepared at the end of the meal to help with some of the clearing up.

Your fellow guests

All kinds of people find their way into monastic *hospederías*. That's one of the main appeals. We've met people who—like us—were curious to discover what it is like to stay in a monastery and experience cloistered life. We've also met people who had come to the monastery to reaffirm their faith—or to find it for the first time. Then, too, we've encountered people who needed a break from the pressures of modern life, and people who were trying to recover from troubled pasts and thought a spell in a monastery would set them on the right path again. These people came from all walks of life. Nearly all of them were Spanish (so far, few tourists find their way into monasteries), but many of them spoke English as it is the *lingua franca* in Spain, just as it is in nearly all European countries.

GETTING IN AND OUT

In all the monasteries we stayed in, we were free to come and go as we pleased—during the day, that is. Typically, we were given a key to our room or cell, along with a key to any interior door that, if locked, would have blocked our access to our room. We were never given a key to a monastery's main door, but during the day the main doors were never locked. It's different at night. The main doors are then typically sealed tight.

Night in a monastery usually begins at 10:00 p.m., so if you're a night owl and prone to carousing, the monastic life might not be for you. After lights out, it's almost impossible to break into a monastery, or to rouse anyone inside who might be willing to let you in.

THE RELIGION THING

You don't have to believe in God to stay in a Spanish monastery, nor do you have to pretend you do. All that's required is that you respect the people who do believe, and that you defer to the rules of the monks and nuns and to their chosen lifestyles and faith. That might mean living more quietly than you normally do. As we discovered, it's a myth that modern-day monks and nuns have taken vows of silence, but they make no unnecessary noise and they are all familiar with biblical passages such as James 1:26, "Those who consider themselves religious, and yet do not keep a tight rein on their tongues, deceive themselves and their religion is worthless," and Proverbs 10:19, "Sin is not ended by multiplying words, but the prudent hold their tongues."

You also need to arrive on time for any of the services you decide to attend—but, of course, you don't need to attend any of the services unless the monastery is open only to those people who are on retreat. If that's the case, you will find out when you try to book a room. You can then decide—at the outset—if you want to stay there or not.

About the Authors

Richard Starks has worked as a writer, editor, and publisher of newsletters and magazines in Canada, the United Kingdom, and the United States. He is the author of six previous books, two co-authored with Miriam Murcutt.

Miriam Murcutt is a writer, editor, and former marketing executive in the travel and publishing industries in Canada, the United Kingdom, and the United States. She has co-authored two other books, both with Richard Starks.

The first book, *Lost in Tibet*, is a true-life adventure set against the political and cultural background of pre-Chinese Tibet. The second, *Along the River that Flows Uphill*, is a travel book that uses

an account of an Amazon journey the authors made to assess the risks inherent in all adventurous travel.

The two authors have travelled extensively throughout Europe, South and Central America, the Far East, and the Himalayas. They rank their journey through Spain's ancient monasteries as one of their most rewarding experiences.

Visit them at www.starksmurcutt.com.